D0828871

THE FATHER
Finding the Perfect
I NEVER
Parent in God
KNEW

PHIL DAVIS

Minnesota Bible College Library
920 Mayowood Rd SW
Rochester, MN 55902
Crossroads College
G.H. Cachiaras Memorial Library
920 Mayowood Road SW, Rochester MN 55902
507-535-3331

NAVPRESS ®
A MINISTRY OF THE NAVIGATORS
P.O. BOX 6000, COLORADO SPRINGS, COLORADO 80934

The Navigators is an international Christian organization. Jesus Christ gave His followers the Great Commission to go and make disciples (Matthew 28:19). The aim of The Navigators is to help fulfill that commission by multiplying laborers for Christ in every nation.

NavPress is the publishing ministry of The Navigators. NavPress publications are tools to help Christians grow. Although publications alone cannot make disciples or change lives, they can help believers learn biblical discipleship, and apply what they learn to their lives and ministries.

© 1991 by Phil Davis
All rights reserved. No part of this publication may be reproduced in any form without written permission from NavPress, P.O. Box 6000, Colorado Springs, CO 80934.
Library of Congress Catalog Card Number: 90-63218
ISBN 08910-96124

Cover illustration: Katherine Mahoney

Unless otherwise identified, all Scripture quotations in this publication are from the *Holy Bible: New International Version* (NIV). Copyright © 1973, 1978, 1984, International Bible Society. Used by permission of Zondervan Bible Publishers. Other versions used include: the *New American Standard Bible* (NASB), © The Lockman Foundation 1960, 1962, 1963, 1968, 1971, 1972, 1973, 1975, 1977; *The New Testament in Modern English* (PH), J. B. Phillips Translator, © J. B. Phillips 1958, 1960, 1972, used by permission of Macmillan Publishing Company; *The Living Bible* (TLB), © 1971 owned by assignment by the Illinois Regional Bank N.A. (as trustee), used by permission of Tyndale House Publishers, Inc., Wheaton, IL 60189; and the *King James Version* (KJV).

Printed in the United States of America

Contents

PART III: Learning to See How God Is Parenting You

To Judy, my wife,
for her "constant faith and abiding love,"
for her endless encouragement,
and for believing in me
when neither I nor others did.

And to my children, Scott, Steve, and Kimberly,
for the part they have played in
teaching me God's love and God's parenting.

Author

Phil Davis is the founding pastor of Lake Mary Community Church, an Evangelical Free Church in the north suburbs of Orlando, Florida. Phil earned a M.Div. from Trinity Evangelical Divinity School, Deerfield, Illinois.

A native of Long Island, New York, Phil became a Christian through a Navigator military ministry while serving in the U.S. Air Force. After several years of involvement with Navigator ministries, churches, and a career job with an aerospace company, he followed God's leading to go to seminary and into full-time ministry.

Phil and his wife, Judy, were married in 1974 and have three children—twin boys, Scott and Steve, and a daughter, Kimberly.

Foreword

The Bible teaches us that God is the heavenly Father of all who trust in Christ. Unfortunately, the word *father* has fallen into some disrepute in recent years. People too often form a conception of God based on their relationship with their earthly father. If their father was stern and demanding, or even angry and abusive, some people will perceive God to be that way.

For a number of years I have been troubled about the tendency, even among Christians, to transfer to God the negative character traits found in fallible, sinful human fathers. To do so is to completely disregard the obvious distinction between sinful human beings and a loving and perfectly righteous God. As people who possess in the Bible the only accurate revelation of God, we need to learn to develop our understanding of the character of God from the Bible, not from the conduct of our earthly fathers.

Therefore, I was encouraged and delighted when I picked up Phil Davis' manuscript and read these words, "I am convicted that we need to be willing to nurture belief in the Bible's teaching of God's image, not in the distorted images [of our fathers] we may have fashioned from childhood."

I share Phil's conviction and commend his book as a helpful contribution toward that goal. Phil has a delightful ability to take ordinary events of life that would pass by most of us and use them as insightful object lessons to teach us about the ways in which God deals with us as His children. More than that, he is faithful to the Scriptures as he presents to us the character of God in His role as our all-wise and all-loving heavenly Father.

I pray that all who read this book will be helped to develop a more biblical view of the character of God.

—JERRY BRIDGES

Acknowledgments

I want to thank my wife, Judy, for cheerfully enduring a series of "crazy" years of seminary, moves, church ministries, and disappointments, all of which contributed to God's training program in my life (and hers). She seemed to have enough faith for both of us when I had my doubts about what God was doing with my life. The completion of this book is as much a testimony to her perseverance as it is to mine. I am grateful to my mom and dad for their positive examples of parental kindness and care.

Thanks to Darrell Sanders for his early input in my life, and then twenty years later, for casually passing on a newsletter that opened the door for this book.

The editors at NavPress . . . Thanks to Bruce Nygren for giving me a chance and for seeing something in a couple of the early (and rough) chapters of this book. Thanks to Karen Hinckley's early advice and midstream adjustments, which made a major difference in the whole project. And a special thanks to Traci Mullins for her encouragement, editorial wisdom, helpful revisions, and kindness to a first-time author.

A special thanks to Lake Mary Community Church, where I am pastoring, for all the support, love, encouragement, and time to work on this book. I am thankful that it is a place where God and His people have let me dream again *and* let me see the fulfillment of many of those dreams.

To God be the glory.

Though I fail, I weep;
Though I halt in pace,
Yet I creep
To the throne of grace.
George Herbert
"Discipline"

"But while he was still a long way off, his father saw
him and was filled with compassion for him; he ran to
his son, threw his arms around him and kissed him."
Jesus Christ
Luke 15:20
from The Parable of the Lost Son

PART I

The Search
for an Ideal Parent

ONE

A Secret Yearning

*For not an orphan in the world can be so deserted as
the child who is an outcast from a living parent's love.*
Charles Dickens
Dombey and Son

In you the fatherless find compassion.
The Prophet Hosea
Hosea 14:3

I threw the hammer down in frustration and stormed out of the house. I was angry with my dad. That was nearly thirty years ago, but the scene flashed back to me recently.

I was twelve, maybe thirteen. I was helping my dad nail down pieces of oak tongue-and-groove flooring in our unfinished attic. We had to make sure we carefully positioned the nails and then make sure we didn't bend the nails or dent the expensive wood. I guess I thought I could do a good job, but the wood was hard and the special nails bent easily for me—not for my dad. He was a good craftsman, and he was trying to make sure I did a good job. I was trying, but I wasn't succeeding.

The attic was hot and stuffy. Dad got upset about every

17

mistake I made, and I grew irritated with him and myself. Finally, I bent one more nail, my dad got mad one more time—I'd had enough. He could do the job himself because I obviously wasn't doing it well enough to satisfy him. So I threw the hammer down, made some irate remark, and left the house for the afternoon.

It was a little moment, quickly forgotten . . . or was it? Sometimes little moments like that stick with you unconsciously. They are not indicative of a whole relationship, but they show an emerging pattern in a person. Between my dad's craftsmanship and my adolescent perfectionism sparks were bound to fly that day in the attic.

At eighteen, I left home to enlist in the U.S. Air Force and never returned home to live. My dad's death, when I was twenty-five, left something unfinished and undeveloped in me. It was not anything he ever said nor even implied, but he died before I felt that I had proven myself to him. I've since learned that I spent many years trying to prove myself to two dads: my earthly father and God, my heavenly Father. As a Christian I spent years never believing that I was quite good enough for God.

Now *I* am a father. One afternoon, while working in the garage with my two eleven-year-old sons, a strange thing happened. I was building a wooden structure for a church project and my sons wanted to help. I knew that I could do the job faster and easier by myself, but I decided to let them hammer a few nails. It wasn't long before it became clear that they weren't doing a good enough job. The nails were bending—making more work for me. I was running out of time and patience, and I let my irritation show by little comments about their lack of ability to do the job correctly. I didn't tell them to leave, but they must have taken the hint.

After they left to play with their friends, I realized what I had done. My perfectionism and impatience got the better of me. I wondered if I was guilty of appearing like a father who thought they never could do a good enough job. I shook my head, remembering some other bent nails on a hot summer day in the attic with my father.

Most of our life revolves around a few themes and long- ings that are common to us all. Whether it's winning appro- val, finding affection, being accepted, becoming satisfied with ourselves, or finding a niche, the themes and longings of our life are set by our personalities, families, parents, friends, schools, and churches. Most of us don't recognize these emerging longings until the themes of our life are already deeply ingrained. Sometimes the real yearnings of our life remain submerged beneath layers of legitimate but sometimes misdirected activity. And many of us do not real- ize how much our fathers and mothers remain with us even after we have left home or they have left this earth.

Losing my father left something unfinished within me, something unresolved. It made me realize how powerful a need I had for a father. Ultimately, it led me to a stron- ger appreciation for my heavenly Father. But it has been a journey.

Many of you reading this have experienced the rejection of your earthly father or mother in one way or another. Per- haps this makes it difficult for you to believe God can be trusted, that He accepts you and loves you. Perhaps this makes it difficult for you to see the rich blessing in the truth that God is your Father.

LOSS OF PARENTAL BEARINGS

In the Stephen Spielberg movie *Empire of the Sun* a boy is separated from his parents in the mayhem on the streets of war-torn China during World War II. (The story is based on the real life experiences of author J. G. Ballard.) The boy winds up in a Japanese internment camp where his need for parents makes him desperate to belong and iden- tify with someone who can fill the void. His busyness, resourcefulness, and desire to please mask his painful loss. As he moves through the movie he attaches himself to people: an American con man, a tired, unloving English couple, and even a Japanese officer. For the boy, the issue is not ideologies and nations. The issue is his need for a sense of parental love and belonging. Eventually, he breaks down and collapses into the arms of an English doctor, crying, "I can't remember what my parents look like."

Parents play such a primary role in a child's need for love, acceptance, and belonging that when they fail or are gone the child becomes desperate to fill the resulting void. The boy in *The Empire of the Sun* was dealing with the sorrow of losing his parental bearings.

Olga was only a child when she lost her father to divorce. She remembers making up stories about him for her classmates who always talked about their fathers. The loss of her father is clearly the major event that shaped her life.

> I really adored my father and was always hoping that my parents would get back together. There was a time when he wanted to come back, but my mother wouldn't go for it. He always made a lot of promises and I always believed him, but she never did. There was a big conflict between my mother and myself, because I had so much confidence in him.
>
> Then, when I was thirteen, he married and moved away, and I've hardly seen him at all since then. When I do see him, it's because I made the effort, and he is always rather indifferent, like I was just an obligation he had, a reminder of his failure. . . . I'm very insecure emotionally, but I am a survivor. . . . I'm just so afraid of being hurt or rejected.[1]

From the orphan boy who yearns for a father to the young man who seeks a fatherly mentor, from the blossoming teenage girl who misses the affection of her withdrawn father to the young woman who marries a man old enough to be her father, we are people who consciously and even unconsciously move through life seeking to find a "father." And though some would sooner forget the image of their father due to abuse, alcoholism, absenteeism, or unlovable characteristics, the need for a good father figure can continue to be a strong motivation throughout their life.

SEARCHING FOR APPROVAL

The reasons we search for a "father" are numerous and sometimes complex. Some search due to an absence of fathering, others because of a negative father figure in the formative years of growth. Whatever the reasons, it is significant that we search and that the need is real. The yearning for a model father is so pervasive that it is my conviction that God placed this need within men and women. But our need will not be realized nor our search ended until we see God as our only adequate Father. It has been said that within everyone there is a God-shaped vacuum that only God can fill. We could also say that within everyone there is a Father-shaped vacuum that only God the Father can fill.

In the book *The Secrets Men Keep*, Dr. Ken Druck (with James C. Simmons) lists the six major areas in which men keep secrets. First on the list is, "Men secretly yearn for their father's love and approval."[2]

Druck writes, "Often they are unaware that 'the search for father' is behind their drive to prove themselves over and over." To write his book, Druck talked with and surveyed hundreds of men. His conclusions point out the prevalence of men's search for a father.

> It may surprise us to know that the most powerful common denominator influencing men's lives today is the relationship we had with our fathers. . . . Of the hundreds of men I have surveyed over the years, perhaps 90 percent admitted they still had strings leading back to their fathers. In other words, they are still looking to their fathers, even though their fathers may have been dead for years, for approval, acceptance, affection, and understanding.[3]

This holds true whether the relationship was good or bad. Isn't it remarkable that some people go through life never quite realizing that they yearn for their father's approval? Perhaps the years of disappointment and the slow erection of walls separate us from the unfulfilled longings of our childhood and adolescence.

Many families live with deep pain. Sometimes this pain is never resolved. Year by year, it takes a toll in the form of bitterness and defeat.

Louie Anderson, the rotund, boyish-looking comedian who does a lot of family humor, wrote a book entitled *Dear Dad.* It is a series of letters written to his alcoholic father after his father died. Though the letters are laced with humor, Anderson deals with the pain and anger of growing up as one of eleven children with an alcoholic father. Anderson wrote the book to come to grips with his anger toward his neglectful dad.

Once a woman came up to him and said, "Oh, you're the comedian who doesn't use the *F*-word." She was referring to his relatively clean act. But like many comedians, Anderson responded with humor derived from pain. He told her, "I use it all the time. *Family.* It's the dirtiest word I know."

The woman laughed and said, "No, not that one." Anderson smiled and said, "I use that one all the time too . . . *Father.* It's right up there with *Family.* Almost interchangeable." Playing along with her he revealed much about his family pain. Anderson was smiling, only because if he wasn't he would have been crying.[4]

When parents betray their children's trust, the pain that begins in childhood can take a huge toll in adulthood. Anderson said that the letters to his father helped him move from anger to forgiveness. But sometimes we cover our pain hoping it will go away. Sometimes by the time we're adults we have lost touch with our secret longings.

In another study done on men and their parents the author discovered the same secret yearning as Druck.

Men do long for fathers who are warm, receptive, physically affectionate and comforting, open and honest about their feelings, and approving and accepting of their sons despite their son's failures. . . . Most sons—almost all—are perpetually disappointed.[5]

The findings are similar for women. Suzanne Fields interviewed hundreds of women while researching her book *Like Father, Like Daughter*. She found again and again that these women yearned for a greater intimacy with their fathers. "This central thesis emerges from hundreds of interviews and questionnaires: *Daddy hides, and we forever seek him, only occasionally flushing him out of his hiding places.*"[6]

Listen to what was said by some of the women in her interviews:

- A thirty-eight-year-old bank teller in North Dakota laments: "He never really asked about me, and I realize now that I have no idea who he really is. What were his dreams and fears and who were the devils that seduced him with whiskey and work, keeping him away from us? When I cut my long, straight hair, changing it to short and curly, he never even noticed."[7]

- A forty-four-year-old office supervisor in Nashville recalls: "Deep down, I know he cared about me. But I wish more than anything that he had been able to express some of that caring to me directly, verbally if not physically. I only wish he had just said the words!"[8]

- A thirty-year-old secretary from Flagstaff, Arizona, had her only heart-to-heart talk with her father after his heart attack. "We had a long conversation early one crack of dawn, down by the lake where my father had gone to recuperate. This was the only time we had ever really had a truly intimate conversation. We talked about how he felt as a father."[9]

- A young Vermont woman who has not seen her father for five years said: "I'm still trying to find the love and unconditional acceptance I never got from him."[10]

♦ Suzanne Fields sums it up poignantly: "But in most of these female recollections there persists a brooding, elegiac lyricism of yearning—yearning always for more, more, more, a hunger for something never quite captured in that secret place in the heart. Instead there is a terrible sadness, an emptiness, or an overwhelming and destructive anger."[11]

"FATHER HUNGER"

When we lose our father early in life (whether due to abandonment, divorce, or death) the need for a father can become an even stronger motivation. Recent studies show that we may go through years attempting to re-create the missing father. This motivation can be so strong that the American Psychoanalytic Association has called the syndrome "father hunger."

In *Father Loss*, Elyce Wakerman conducted studies and interviews with women who lost their fathers before the age of eighteen. The author found that the loss of a father shapes a girl's life and all her future relationships.

Wakerman recounts the loss of her own father when she was only three years old. She describes her need to be "Daddy's girl" to someone. In speaking for others like herself, she writes with a sense of sadness:

Whether he died or abandoned us, we felt rejected. Despite, perhaps because of, this betrayal, *he remained an indomitable* force within us, *an idealized standard* against which all else would be measured, and found wanting. (emphasis added)[12]

Isak Dinesen, the Danish writer and adventurer whose memoirs in *Out of Africa* were dramatized in the Oscar-winning movie, was nine years old when her father killed himself. Her biographer says that his death was the "central drama" of her existence and his image fueled her inspiration. In a letter to her mother later in life, Dinesen wrote,

"If I can . . . make something of myself again, and can look at life calmly and clearly one day—then it is Father who has done it for me. . . . Often I get the feeling that he is beside me, helping me."[13] Isak's idealization of her father is typical among many who have lost their fathers early.

In studying the lives of famous women of achievement who lost their fathers through death, divorce, or abandonment, Wakerman concludes that "one comes time and again to the influence of an absent father and a nearly conscious search for his approval."[14] She points out,

> Nearly one third of the women who have been married to United States presidents, and five of the nine most recent "first ladies," [up to Reagan] lost their fathers early in life owing to either death or divorce. Behind every great man, there is a great woman, we are told. Behind many of these women, there is a man [a father] that got away.[15]

But the opposite effect can occur also. A British study on the population of women's prisons revealed that more than one third of the prisoners were fatherless.[16] Sociological studies done on inner-city ghettos often correlate the high juvenile crime rate to the absence of fathers and the subsequent single-parent, maternal-figure homes.

From praises to laments, from idealism to disillusionment, the chorus of voices attests to the powerful role "father" plays in our lives.

The need for a father is not simply the search for a "daddy" (or a man to bring home the bread); it is the search for what a good father provides for his child:

- ◆ Acceptance.
- ◆ Affirmation.
- ◆ Authority.
- ◆ Discipline.
- ◆ A sense of security.
- ◆ Warm affection and love.

♦ Trust.
♦ Exemplary behavior.
♦ Values.
♦ Leadership.

Yet the sad truth is that many people never find the love, approval, acceptance, and security they desire.

THE PROMISE OF PERFECT FATHERING

J. Paul Getty, Sr., was one of the wealthiest men in the world. Yet his son J. Paul Getty, Jr., said he seldom saw his father. It is tragic when the rich succeed in leaving a legacy of wealth and prestige to their family, but fail to leave them a legacy of love. Once, while in high school, the young Paul wrote his dad a letter. His father returned it with the spelling and grammatical errors corrected but without a single personal comment. Paul, Jr., confesses, "I never got over that. . . . I wanted to be judged as a human being and I could never get that from him."[17]

Scripture seems to imitate life in the absence of healthy father-son relationships. Other than Jesus Christ and the heavenly Father and the gracious homecoming given to the prodigal son by his loving father, Scripture lacks exemplary father-son relationships. I tried to think of good fatherly examples in Scripture.

We see little of Abraham and Isaac's relationship other than the aborted sacrifice on Mount Moriah. Certainly Isaac's relationships with his sons, Jacob and Esau, were not exemplary. Samuel was given away by his mother to be a priest. Eli seems to have failed as a father with his two sons. Though Jonathan is committed to his father, Saul is hardly an exemplary father. Though David's son Solomon became a great king, we do not see David's relationship with Solomon. Instead, we see the scandalous rebellion of another son of David, Absalom, toward his father.

Scripture tells us that God is *like* a father. But if God is like a father, then where are the good examples? If God is like a father, then why do so many people have negative reference points? Why do so many people deal with the trauma of being orphaned instead of fathered?

Into this void of fatherlessness and "father hunger" two verses in Scripture hold out a promise: "In you the fatherless find compassion" (Hosea 14:8), and "I will not leave you as orphans" (John 14:18). God knows the deepest longings of our hearts.

I remember when my own dad died, I was concerned about my younger brothers growing up without a father. At the time I was twenty-five, married, and had lived away from home for seven years. Though my father's death hurt deeply, and I was depressed and sad for a few months, I was not as concerned for myself as I was for my ten-, fourteen-, and twenty-one-year-old brothers, and of course, my mother.

I remember being comforted by promises from Scripture that said God took a special interest in widows and the fatherless (Psalm 68:5, Isaiah 63:16). So I committed my family to the God of the widows and fatherless.

I don't know that we ever get over the death of a father or mother, especially good ones. I know I have felt the void of my father's absence repeatedly, and I look forward to meeting him again in eternity.

But at the time I did not realize my own need for God to be my Father, my heavenly Father. Not until years later would I begin to appreciate the richness of the image of God as my perfect Father. As the years roll on, the richness of that truth must sink deeper and deeper into my conscious image of God. As a Christian, I have found that this relationship with the Lord has been a journey for me, God's son, to the heart of my heavenly Father.

One of my greatest gifts in this journey is my three children: Steve, Scott, and Kimberly. By becoming a father, God has allowed me to get in touch with a father's heart. In my children, I am often reminded of myself before God. Many nights I have checked on them before I have gone to bed. I've stood by their beds while they lay asleep and thought how much I love them. I often hear God challenge me in response, "If you love your children this much, Phil, how much greater is my love for you and for them?"

Our earthly parent-child bonds can be a great blessing in helping us see God. But even the best human fathers will fail us.

As hard as I try to be a good father to my children, I sometimes blow it. I remember one instance in particular. It was over one of those little things that seems to slip away unnoticed until it's too late. The boys would usually ask me as I hugged them goodnight, "Dad, would you pray for us?" I liked it when they asked, and I would pray for each of them.

Time went on and I realized one night that I had not been praying for them at bedtime. Schedules, late nights, distractions, or laziness seemed to disrupt the routine. But I also realized that they had stopped asking me to pray for them. That's what hurt. That's when I felt that I had failed them. Had my inconsistency caused them to become disinterested? Had my failure to initiate quenched their desire for prayer? I was saddened, and blamed myself that they no longer asked, "Dad, would you pray for us?" They should not have had to ask to begin with.

I guess I am like a lot of paranoid parents: I wonder if I am doing enough of the right things for my children. I wonder how my deficiencies as a parent will affect them. But I am not a perfect parent. God is. This situation helped me realize that God is a more faithful Father than I am. How thankful I am for that! God does not get bogged down by schedules and business. He does not let distractions or laziness disrupt His faithfulness to His children.

Since human fathers—try as they may—still fail, we need to learn to place our ultimate security in God. Unless we find rest in the biblical truth of God being our perfect, heavenly Father we either will be forever searching for a human father to meet needs only God can meet, or we will be emotionally scarred by the painful memories of unsatisfactory fathers who failed us.

TWO

God Is a Dad, Too!

When I was a little kid, a father was like a light in the refrigerator. Every house had one, but no one really knew what either of them did once the door was shut.
Erma Bombeck

In all their distress he too was distressed.
The Prophet Isaiah
Isaiah 63:9

"**H**ey, Dad, wanna have a catch?"
I remember saying those words many times as a boy, anxious to toss the baseball with my dad in our yard. But when I heard them recently at the end of a heartwarming movie they brought back a whole wave of memories and emotions. I was watching the movie for the second time on my VCR. It was late at night. Everyone was in bed, and I was alone.

This movie is about an Iowa farmer who builds a base-ball field in his corn field and meets some unusual "ghosts." Like Dickens's *A Christmas Carol* with its ghost of Christmas past or Capra's *It's a Wonderful Life* with Jimmy Stewart's glimpse at what might have been, every once in a while Hollywood spins a magical yarn that strikes familiar chords

29

in us all. It wasn't the theology of this movie that attracted me; it was the theme of reconciling the "ghosts" of our past. In this story, the young man's father has been dead for a number of years. But the son had never satisfactorily reconciled himself with his dad.

In the closing scene of *Field of Dreams* the young man gets to meet his father as a young baseball player in his twenties. He had known his father only as an old man who had been worn down by the years. But now father and son get to spend time together, young man to young man. The last lines of the movie struck such a familiar chord with me that the tears came easily. As the father begins to walk away, the son says to him boyishly, his voice cracking with emotion, "Hey, Dad, wanna have a catch?" His dad smiles and says with similar emotion, "Yeah, I'd like that." As the son reaches for a baseball glove, picks up a ball, and tosses it to his dad, we know that this is more than just a movie about baseball. It's a reminder of unfinished business, making peace with our past, reconciling with our parents. It's about getting beyond all the stops and starts of parent-child relationships due to misunderstandings and immaturity. This movie reminds us of our desire to capture the special bond between father and child.

It reminded me again that unfinished business and unresolved relationships with parents can carry over into our relationship with God the Father. And our father does not have to be deceased. For many people whose fathers are alive, something in their relationship remains unfinished and unresolved. The relationship hasn't brought all that they would have liked. Human parents will fail us, but our concern here is how those failures and disappointments may have carried over into our view of God being our Father. I have already stated that I felt my father's death left something unfinished in me—that's why I related to the movie so well. Let me explain a little further.

I grew up in the baby-boomer generation, among the ranks of children of middle-class suburbanites who bought look-alike homes in huge developments erected on once-productive potato farms on Long Island, New York. We were fed and cared for by well-meaning parents. My mom and dad made us feel rich, though when I became an adult I realized we weren't. I was fortunate because my parents were kind, loving, and understanding. If God was like my parents, then God was good. But like a spoiled child who isn't thankful enough and takes his parents for granted, I took God for granted. He was there, but I had other interests. I called on Him only when I needed Him.

Like most teenagers, I was not particularly close to my dad during those troublesome years. I joined the Air Force after high school during the Vietnam War. After my four years of Air Force duty (mostly in Florida), I went home to New York for a month, then left to live in Florida. I moved to Florida to go to college and to be involved in a Christian ministry. During the next few years I met my wife in Florida, bought my first home, and visited my family in New York only at Christmas. Three years after my discharge from the Air Force my dad died. He had never seen my Florida home, barely knew my wife, would never see me graduate from college or seminary, would never hear me preach a sermon, and would never know his grandchildren.

Shortly before he died I spent a week visiting him as he lay in the hospital. I saw him accept Christ as his Savior two weeks before his death. He said to me during that time that it really hurt him when I left home to live in Florida after I got out of the Air Force. I was surprised because I never knew that it mattered to him. But there was something that he never said. I didn't realize this until years later, but I never heard my father say, "I'm proud of you, son."

As I think back, maybe there wasn't much to be proud of at that time. I was an above-average student in high school but not an outstanding student. I wasn't on any of the varsity baseball, basketball, or soccer teams. I wasn't in band and just missed being in the honor society. I postponed college to enlist in the Air Force because I didn't know what I wanted to do. My father died before I finished college or decided to "do something with my life" to give him reason to be proud. Somehow, since I hadn't met all of my self-imposed, culturally shaped standards of achievement, I felt that I had never proven myself to him.

Unconsciously, I carried these standards into my Christianity and my view of God being a Father. I felt I had to prove myself to God my Father in order for Him to be proud of me.

Unfinished business with earthly parents can color all of life. For some people the lack of peace with their parents can reflect their lack of peace in life and with God. The connection between the two can be powerful.

How would you complete the following statement?

"I never got the _____ that I wanted from my father."

Acceptance, approval, affection, love, respect . . . which did you choose as the answer? As you read the illustrations think about how parental denial can color our lives as adults.

THE SEARCH FOR FATHERLY APPROVAL

Marvin Gaye, Jr., churned out hit record after hit record during the sixties and seventies, songs like, "I Heard it Through the Grapevine" and "Ain't no Mountain High Enough." But in all his fame and success, his father's love and respect eluded him. A friend once asked Marvin, "Do you love your father?" He answered in a light and confident tone, "Yes." The friend asked, "Then why don't you tell him?" "I can't," Marvin replied.

At one point when Motown Records was due to renew his contract, he demanded a one-million-dollar bonus in cash in a briefcase. He told a friend, "I want a million dollars cash so I can take it to my father and say, 'See that? That's a million dollars. I just want you to know how successful I am.'"

Marvin Gaye, age forty-five, was living with his parents in 1984 when his father, Marvin Gaye, Sr., seventy, shot

him to death after a minor argument. It was April Fools'
Day. A friend recounted, "Marvin told me he never got the
love from his father that he wanted."[1]

Much has been written about the short, unhappy life
of Sylvia Plath, author of the largely autobiographical work
The Bell Jar. She was a prize-winning author before she was
twenty years old, a famous poet, and a college professor.
Born in New England in 1933, Sylvia's life was shaped by
the sudden death of her father when she was eight. Years
later in her journal she would write,

> I rail and rage against the taking of my father, whom
> I have never known; even his mind, his heart, his face
> as a boy of 17 I love terribly . . . I lust for the knowing
> of him. . . .
>
> Me, I never knew the love of a father, the love of a
> steady blood-related man after the age of eight . . . the
> only man who'd love me steady through life; (Mother)
> came in one morning with tears . . . in her eyes and
> told me he was gone for good. I hate her for that.[2]

Sylvia married and had two children. She confessed
that her husband was a substitute for her father. Her mar-
riage ended in divorce, and like many women today she
developed a love-hate relationship toward men.

> I hated men because they didn't stay around and love
> me like a father: . . . Men, nasty, lousy men. They
> took all they could get and then had temper tantrums
> or died or went off to Spain like Mrs. So-and-so's
> husband with his lusty lips. . . .
>
> All my life I have been "stood up" emotionally by
> the people I love most: Daddy dying and leaving me,
> Mother, somehow not there.[3]

Amidst her gloom and her desire for genuine fatherly
love, she visited her father's grave. "Went to my father's
grave . . . I found that flat stone. 'Otto E. Plath: 1885-1940,'
right beside the path, where it would be walked over. Felt

cheated. My temptation to dig him up. To prove he existed and really was dead."[4]

Four months after her separation from her husband, Sylvia committed suicide. She was only thirty. It was not the first time she had tried. After her first attempt, she revealed in a poem, entitled "Daddy," her desire to get back to her father. "At twenty I tried to die and get back, back, back to you. I thought even the bones would do."[5]

Some people carry family pain to their grave. Parents play such a major role in our view of ourself that often the deep longings of our life are set in motion at an early age. Marvin Gaye's longing for his father's acceptance and approval and Sylvia Plath's longing for a father's intimacy and love are tragic versions of many people's yearnings. How can we have a healthy view of God as our Father when so many people remember the rejection, disapproval, or coldness of their human father? There are helpful contrasts. . . .

After a tennis career filled with highlights and accomplishments, Chris Evert, then thirty-four, retired after her loss in the quarterfinals of the U.S. Open in 1989. The newspapers revealed the following day that beyond all the glory, money, boyfriends, and fans, Chris Evert had "always played tennis to please her father."[6] Her father was the first to reach her after her final match.

Race car driver Bobby Allison could fill a room with all the trophies he's won. But in 1989 after a career-ending mishap left Allison with head injuries and a shortened memory, it was his son Davey's turn in the spotlight at Daytona's Firecracker 400. His dad had finished first in this contest for the previous six years. But at the close of the race, twenty-eight-year-old winner Davey Allison sank teary-eyed and jubilant into the arms of his legendary father. Fighting back tears, the son said, "I can't thank you enough for all you've done for me. . . . This one's for you, Dad."[7]

Margaret Thatcher regretted that her father never lived to see her become either a cabinet minister or Prime Minister of Great Britain. But the day she became Prime Minister she paid tribute to her father.

He brought me up to believe all the things I do
believe. . . . It's passionately interesting to me that
the things I learned in a small town, in a very mod-
est home, are just the things that I believe have
won the election. . . . I owe almost everything to my
father.[8]

Moments like these remind us that the bond between
children and parents tugs at all of our heartstrings. The
parental bond is a marvelous aspect of humanness; our
Creator has designed human beings with the capacity and
need for deep parental bonding. Yet this earthly parent-
child relationship serves as a promise of an even greater
spiritual relationship that we have been called into by the
Most High God, who is our heavenly Father. That fatherly
approval, acceptance, and love can be found in Him. God
our Father offers us a Parent-child relationship more satisfying and vital than any here on earth.

Many Christians know a lot of Scripture and have heard
many sermons. Yet, if you are like me, sometimes Scripture
can remain in a cerebral realm for years before it actually
engages the heart with dynamic force. We know intellectually that God is our Father, but deep down we are not too
comfortable with that idea. All of us have had less-than-
perfect parents (some outright evil) so to that extent all of
us have had distorted models of our Father God. But for us
to truly love and worship and serve God, we need to see His
tenderness, concern, personableness, approachability, and
Fatherly heart. For me, entering into God's heart has come
through knowing Scripture as the Holy Spirit has used circumstances to bring that truth to life in my sometimes dull
and leathery heart.

EMERGENCY ROOM: SCENE ONE

I sat on one gurney in the emergency room looking at my
son lying on another gurney, both of us waiting for medical
treatment. Scott's injury definitely was an emergency. He

needed a few stitches in a laceration on his scalp. My injury wasn't an emergency, but for a few days I had suspected I needed treatment. I had developed a big knot on my elbow from falling on it in a basketball game. I knew what Scott needed; I didn't know what they would do to me. I hoped all the elbow needed was a draining. But I wished I could have taken Scott's place because I knew his injury was more painful than mine.

I watched and winced and comforted Scott in his pain while he peered out from under a blue, sterile cloth covering his head. He squeezed my fingers till his fingers were white as the doctor stuck a needle in the wound. I couldn't watch because I knew how much it hurt. He didn't scream or cry; he just winced, nervously twitched his legs, and clamped down hard on my fingers.

After it was over, it was Dad's turn. Scott watched and winced as the physician stuck a thick needle in my elbow and left it for a few minutes while the liquid and blood drained out.

I hate needles, especially thick ones. But a father has to be extra calm as his eight-year-old son watches him under pressure. Especially since moments earlier, while the son was undergoing treatment, the father was comforting him with lines like, "It's okay, son. Don't worry; it won't hurt."

This scene took on a special meaning for me that afternoon. Somehow, "Dad" sitting there in the emergency room with a real injury, sharing a similar pain, and going through it *with* Scott made it easier for him. I didn't deny my pain; I told Scott it hurt, but it wasn't that bad. I couldn't help thinking that in some small way this emergency-room scene was allowing me to take a glimpse into a profound mystery that is played out in the lives of God the Father and His children.

I've been in emergency rooms on the other side of the injury, as a corpsman in the military. I've worked in hospitals, driven ambulances, and helped emergency-room doctors as they stitched up patients. I've stepped around, over, and in puddles of blood on emergency room floors. But this was my first time as a parent. Somehow my son's minor laceration was worse than the gory wounds of unknown patients. I felt in those moments that I entered into the heart of God in a way I still marvel at. I experienced the reality of God being "with" me from a father's viewpoint.

The truth hit home in that moment in a way it never had before in all my reading, in all my theology classes, and in all the messages I'd heard. I had always known as a believer that God had suffered *for* us in the Atonement. But the reality that God suffers as our heavenly Father *along with* us in the midst of our pain suddenly illuminated God's Fatherhood in a rich warmth.

I have often thought that God suffered only once—on the cross. But as for humans, we suffer often and repeatedly. I have often pondered the implications of Christ being our "Emmanuel"—God *with* us. To what extent is He "with" me? I've asked, "Does He really enter into my pain and suffering, or is He just there as an observer?" In moments of frustration, I have accused God of being indifferent to my pain and lacking compassion. "Why doesn't He take away my pain and hurt and suffering?" I have wished that He was more involved with the inner turmoil of my life and in so doing assigned Him to a monkish sort of existence in which He moves only among the "spiritual" catacombs of my life. I have not seen Him as an involved Father, but almost as an absentee Father. Like the father who seems always hidden behind the outspread pages of the newspaper in his favorite chair or at the table, at times my God seemed to remain distant behind the pages of my Bible.

But there in the emergency room God melted my stubborn image. There I realized He is a Father, more loving and compassionate than I could ever be as a human father. It was as if He stood beside me there in the emergency room and calmly said, "You see the way you hurt for and with your son? In the same way I hurt and suffer with you, My son, for I am your Father."

Although God, after suffering *for our sins* on the cross, cannot suffer *in our place* in life, He does hurt *with* us as a Father with His children. We must go through it, but He goes through it with us.

We can take comfort in knowing He is there peering at us under the blue cloth, and we can look on in amazement at His wounds: "In all their distress he too was distressed" (Isaiah 63:9).

EMERGENCY ROOM: SCENE TWO

Three weeks later, Scott and I were back at the same hospital. We were in the same room, on the same gurney, with the same doctor and the same diagnosis. This time, however, Scott needed three stitches in his head instead of four. And this time I was simply the parent instead of a fellow patient.

There was the certain added frustration Scott and I felt that this injury happened again. It was the frustration of being a patient again and needing treatment again and going through the same pain again. But God was teaching me again also. Once again I saw my son as God sees me, His son.

I thought as I sat there looking at Scott's sad, distraught face, *We've been through this before. But that doesn't make it any easier or less painful, does it, son?* It wasn't the first time I had muttered those thoughts that day.

Earlier that day I had been going through a bout of sadness and reflection . . . ironically, I was feeling like a patient before God. And I was feeling the frustration of being in recurring, familiar inner pain in my own heart and spirit. You must know how it is, for most believers on occasion have recurring problems, doubts, sins, temptations, or fears. For me, that day, it had been a sense of regret that I still struggled with some recurring fears and doubts about God's faithfulness to me. I had doubted His real commitment to help me, a struggling pastor. *Why can't I get this settled, Lord? Why can't I be more restful in believing You love me? Why can't I get beyond these nagging doubts? I should be more mature than this. I should have settled this by now.* Caught between real fears and a lack of perspective, I also began upbraiding myself for my self-pity and my inability to "snap out of it." As fears and doubts snowball in us we often feel further condemned by them and wonder how and why God puts up with us.

In the midst of all this, I believed God too must have been acknowledging to me, *We've been here before. We've gone through this before, son.* The same escalating fears, the same painful sense of rejection. And responding to God in prayer I had muttered, "But that doesn't make it any easier." An inner hurt and pain can wear us down; it can debilitate the spirit and deflate our hope and joy. Like a needy patient with a recurring wound, I was frustrated with myself for being spiritually clumsy and slow to heal.

There are times when we are like patients before the Lord. Sometimes we need minor surgery, sometimes major surgery, and sometimes we need a period of convalescence to help us gain strength to get back up on our feet.

So as I leaned over Scott, my son, as he lay on the emergency-room bed, and as I peered once again at him under the sterilized blue cloth, I saw the drama being played out between Father and son, between God and me. I am the child, and God the Father leans over me to comfort and encourage me in my recurring injuries, pain, and need. It would be unthinkable for me to abandon my son in his time of need. God is our Father. God is my Father. He does not abandon me when I make the same dumb mistake and wind up injured again. There are times for discipline, and there are times for comfort; the good parent knows the difference.

How many times have I missed the point about God's Fatherly love? How many times have I belittled His love and degraded His greatness and Fatherly care by imagining Him to be less of a Father to me than I am to my children? How many times have I imagined Him as One who quickly rejects me upon the slightest fault and who does not tolerate my spiritual immaturity? How many times have I essentially made the estimation that I am a better parent to my children than God is to me?

Those trips to the emergency room capsulized for me a parent's vantage point as he deals with his children. And in playing the role of a parent I am repeatedly privileged to get a better glimpse of the heart of God as He is a Parent to me.

God is much more involved with His children than we realize. Though He is transcendent, omnipotent, and the incomprehensible Holy Other, it does not cause Him to be stoical and unmoved. God is also immanent: close to, with, and dwelling in His people. Though Scripture uses figurative terms and analogies to describe God in human language, that does not mean God is merely superhuman in His qualities. It uses such language to communicate truth about the nature of God. We may not understand how an infinite God's emotions differ from man's, but Scripture affirms that God has emotions (He grieves, can be distressed, experiences sorrow and delight). It says of Christ, "We do not have a high priest who is unable to sympathize with our weaknesses" (Hebrews 4:15).

The promise from the Old Testament was that God would dwell with His people, that He would be their "Emmanuel." How we need this assurance! We need the reality of God dwelling with us to burst upon our hearts as a fresh reminder of His deep personal involvement.

THREE

Abba, Father

Everyone is born to be an orphan.
Saul Bellow

"I will not leave you as orphans; I will come to you."
Jesus Christ
John 14:18

My friend told me about becoming an orphan. He had many run-ins with the police before his mother finally abandoned him when he was seven. He was placed in a juvenile detention center and often spent time in solitary confinement, even at age seven. Undernourished, rebellious, and untrusting of adults, he was on course to becoming a miserable adult. But God reached out to him there in the orphanage through an old man who led him to the Lord. My friend remembers how before his adoption he and the other orphans would talk about finding the perfect home and family. He remembers praying that God would give him "new parents," he didn't want the "old ones" back; within a short time, he was adopted by a wealthy, influential couple.

The plight of orphans touches a special place in our hearts. Their neediness is so apparent to us.

I was surprised to find how many influential world leaders were orphans. Paul Tournier in his book *Creative Suffering* writes that Dr. Pierre Rentchnick compiled a list of over three hundred of the most famous people in history who were orphans. These people lost either one or both parents early in life, or were abandoned, or were illegitimate children who did not know their fathers. The list reads like a who's who of world history: Alexander the Great, Julius Caesar, Charles V, Cardinal Richelieu, Louis XIV, George Washington, Napoleon, Queen Victoria, Golda Meir, Hitler, Lenin, Stalin, Eva Peron, Fidel Castro. Rentchnick also included great religious leaders: Buddha, Mohammed, Confucius.

The list does not stop with political and religious leaders. Many writers, philosophers, and artists were orphans: Rudyard Kipling, Leo Tolstoy, Albert Camus, Voltaire, Pascal, Dostoevsky, Rousseau, Sartre, Bertrand Russell, Johann Sebastian Bach, Charles Dickens, Charlotte Brontë. Paul Tournier, Christian author and counselor, lost both his parents by age five. Writers and artists have a particular gift for being able to give creative expression to their emotional trauma and hardships of life. They are keenly aware of losses, and their sensitive spirits help them convey to others the pain of being human.

Tournier writes that Rentchnick's own book—*Do Orphans Lead the World?*—links the emotional deprivation of these orphans to a desire to be in control, which drove them to positions of authority in order to transform the world for better or worse. Sometimes we may imagine orphans as deprived underachievers, but the evidence challenges this stereotype.

Yet Tournier reminds us, "For the few hundreds of orphans listed by Rentchnick who have made a name for themselves in history, there are millions whom deprivation in childhood has handicapped for life."[1]

At times in history, the numbers of orphans have been tragically high. During the time of the Roman Empire, orphans and unwanted children often died from neglect, were killed, or were sold into slavery. On one occasion in the twelfth century, Innocent III was appalled when he arrived in Rome and saw the number of babies' bodies floating in the Tiber River. Prior to the Reformation, convents and monasteries regularly cared for unwanted and orphaned children. During the Industrial Revolution their population exploded, and cities were full of street urchins and waifs. After the American Civil War, city orphanage asylums multiplied to meet the need. From the late 1800s through the turn of the century, "orphan trains" loaded with children for adoption carted orphans from the eastern cities to the farms out West.

No wonder God, in His great foresight, told us that He had a special interest in orphans. He knew how many there would be! When Scripture promises that in God "the fatherless find compassion" (Hosea 14:3), it shows that God knows the great vacuum within us that yearns for parental love and care.

EMOTIONAL AND SPIRITUAL ORPHANS

The great Russian writer Leo Tolstoy lost his mother when he was very young. Yet at age eighty he wrote a belated orphan cry in his journal: "Yes, yes, my Maman, whom I was never able to call that because I did not know how to talk when she died. She is my highest image of love—not cold, divine love, but warm, earthly love, maternal. . . . Maman, hold me, baby me! . . . All this is madness, but it is true."[2]

Parents symbolize the longing for love, affection, belonging, and worth acutely felt within orphans. Bertrand Russell, the noted philosopher, lost both parents at an early age. The experience of being an orphan fueled one of the great passions of his life: "the longing for love."[3]

Orphans give us a symbolic picture of man in need. Perhaps that is what led writer Saul Bellow to say, "Everyone is born to be an orphan."[4]

You and I don't have to be orphans to know the desire for

a "perfect" family, and the "ideal" mother and father. Many who were never abandoned or orphaned by their earthly parents are emotionally and spiritually orphans, searching for someone to give them love, belonging, worth, and security. Those of us who found Christ, or were found by Him, are just as needy. Many adopted sons and daughters in God's family remain emotionally and spiritually orphaned because they fail to know the fatherly and motherly comforts of their heavenly Parent.

Noreen, who shared her thoughts with me at length, has given me permission to tell part of her story:

> I felt like I really didn't have any parents. With my father being angry and sexually abusive and my mother being passive and not affectionate, I grew up emotionally deprived and starved for attention. I knew other families were more "normal." I'd watch television and dream of having parents like Ozzie and Harriet Nelson or Donna Reed, you know, the ideal families. Today, I look at my little daughter and see how cute and cheerful she is and remember that as a child I felt so ugly and unlovable. It is amazing I didn't wind up a prostitute out on the streets. But God was watching over me in a special way. I got the attention and approval I needed from my teachers, and that helped a lot. I remember falling asleep at night wondering if anyone would ever love me and think I was pretty.

Noreen's story is not unusual; it is the experience of many. It reminds us of the crying needs within. And it also demonstrates, as we will see, that God is faithful. Our Savior's words get right to the core when He says, "I will not leave you as orphans; I will come to you" (John 14:18). He was not speaking these words to literal "children." He was talking to grown men with fear and anxiety and lostness written all over their faces. Jesus was speaking to the disciples during their last evening together when He made this promise. The *New International Version* and the *New American Standard Bible* capture the real sense of the word He used. It is, quite literally, the equivalent to our word *orphan* (the Greek word is *orphanos*). Jesus knew that the emotional trauma associated with being orphaned was particularly descriptive of the spiritual needs of His disciples at that moment and of men and women today, centuries later. It is this need that God the Father intends to meet through Christ, who promises to send us the "Comforter" (John 14:16, KJV), the Holy Spirit, to dwell within and give the perpetual witness of God's presence and our sonship.

The great promise of the coming Messiah in Isaiah 9:6 gives us a potent description of various aspects of the character of God: "He will be called Wonderful Counselor, Mighty God, Everlasting Father, Prince of Peace." God is not a Father who abandons us, who fails us, who is coldly distant. Our God is an everlasting Father. This is not a role He takes upon Himself periodically; this is His nature. When Jesus taught His disciples to pray, He taught them to address God as "Father."

What we are *not* told to do is often significant. Jesus could have had us address God by a title descriptive of other aspects of His character. He could have had us address God as "Our Savior" (as Paul addressed God in 1 Timothy 1:1, 2:3), expressing God's great plan of redemption. He could have had us address God as the "Almighty One," emphasizing God's power. Or any of the Old Testament titles: the Holy One of Israel, the Most High God, the Lord of Hosts, the Lord God, or Yahweh. But Jesus gave them and us a more personal, more relational way in which to address the Lord God Almighty: "Father."

ADOPTION

For those who acknowledge the pain and loneliness of spiritual and emotional orphanhood, the invitation to become the beloved child of a faithful heavenly Father promises to satisfy their most raging internal hunger. But is this perfect relationship within their reach? How can a searching orphan child find what he or she longs for?

An orphan needs to be *adopted*. God made provisions for this, and the Bible speaks of salvation as being adopted into God's family. Paul says, "He predestined us to *adoption* as sons through Jesus Christ to Himself, according to the kind intention of His will" (Ephesians 1:5, NASB; emphasis added). Though Scripture uses the word *adoption* only a few times, it has heavy theological content.

> For you have not received a spirit of slavery leading to fear again, but you have received a spirit of adoption as sons by which we cry out, "Abba, Father!" (Romans 8:15, NASB)

> God sent forth His Son . . . in order that He might redeem those who were under the Law, that we might receive the adoption as sons. And because you are sons, God has sent forth the Spirit of His Son into our hearts, crying, "Abba! Father!" (Galatians 4:4-6, NASB)

Both of these passages speak of *receiving* adoption into God's family and link adoption to personal endearment with God in addressing Him as "Abba, Father." The Greek word for adoption (used in these two passages) actually has the Greek word for "son" as its prefix. Adoption meant becoming a son, a part of the family, granted an inheritance as an heir. (The NIV chooses to translate the Greek word for "adoption" in Romans 8:15 and Galatians 4:5 differently. Instead, it substitutes "Spirit of sonship" and "full rights as sons," respectively. These expressions, while helpful, lose the distinctiveness of the word *adoption.*)

Adoption is a special concept because it shows the deliberate choice that the Father makes. J. I. Packer writes,

> Adoption is a *family* idea, conceived in terms of *love*, and viewing God as a *Father*. In adoption, God takes us into his family and fellowship, and establishes us

as his children and heirs. Closeness, affection, and generosity are at the heart of the relationship. To be right with God the judge is a great thing, but to be loved and cared for by God the Father is a greater.[5]

It is helpful to see the richness of the family metaphors that Paul uses in his epistles. Paul's use of terms such as *adoption, inheritance,* and *heirs* may not sound appealing. They are more than just words with a sentimental "family" meaning, these words had legal meaning in Paul's day. He used them to enhance the technical and theological meaning of our status as children of God.

Paul was a Roman citizen and was familiar with the extensive legal system. Paul used terms such as adoption, inheritance, and heirs in his epistles with Roman connections because his readers would have been most familiar with Roman law.[6]

In a Roman household (or family) the father was the head and heart of the family, and his power was "all-pervasive."[7] There is a continuity between fathers and children. There was no "coming of age" at which the "child" obtained independence as a matter of right. It would be quite possible for a mature and even an old man to be by law still the child of his father and subject to his authority.[8]

This was not meant to be restrictive and negative, but rather to be a meaningful connectedness between children and their fathers. So when Paul says to the Ephesians that they are "members of God's household" (2:19), it is not just a nice expression.

Professor Francis Lyall, in his extensive study of legal metaphors *Slaves, Citizens, Sons,* says that the Roman adoption laws were much more extensive and relationship-oriented than either Greek adoption laws or Hebrew concepts of adoption (which were virtually unheard of).

There were two different adoption procedures (*adrogatio* and *adoptio*) both of which brought a person into a new family and made him a member in virtually all respects. One of these two forms (adrogatio) made a person a member of a new family by canceling all his debts and obligations but did not put him under the legal authority of another person. The second form of adoption (adoptio) was more inclusive and put the adoptee under "the legal power and authority of another."[9] This later form is closest to Paul's use of the adoption metaphor.

This second form of Roman adoption had a two-stage procedure. Under Roman law the first stage involved the destruction of the paternal power of the previous father. The second stage involved the new relationship with a new father and the establishment of his fatherly power. With this background we can see why Paul would have used *adoption* to communicate theological concepts.

Being adopted was much more than merely being a foster child. Being adopted brought about a change in a person's natural parents, new parents, and his or her own status as a child. Spiritually we are adopted by God, and we are no longer children of darkness but children of a heavenly Father. We are not merely foster children who do not really become a part of a family, but we are adopted children who are legally part of a new family.

The profound truth of Roman adoption was that the adoptee was taken out of his previous state and was placed in a new relationship of son to his new father. All of his old debts were canceled, and in effect the adoptee started a new life as part of his new family. From that time on the father (or *paterfamilias*) had the same control over his new "child" as he had over his natural offspring. He owned all the property and acquisitions of the adoptee, controlled his personal relationships, and had rights of discipline. On the other hand, the father was liable for the actions of the adoptee, and each owed the other reciprocal duties of support and maintenance.[10]

Two other legal terms appear in Paul's "Roman" epistles, *heir* and *inheritance*. In Scripture *inheritance* in the broadest sense "encompasses the whole of God's goodness to man."[11] By most law a person isn't an heir until his ancestor dies, but by Roman law "birth not death constituted heirship."[12]

In Roman law there was a "continuity of personality between heir and ancestor."[13]

Gaius, early writer of Roman law, wrote that the children "even in their father's lifetime are considered in a manner owners."[14] When Paul says that we are "heirs—heirs of God and joint-heirs with Christ" (Romans 8:17), he wants us to know that we are co-owners now with God and Christ of all of the divine inheritance. To be an heir of God does not mean we are waiting for some future point when someone dies, we are joint-owners here and now, and there is a "continuity of personality"—a vital connectedness between the believer and God the Father.

"Adoption" is God reaching out to needy man: orphaned and parentless, without the vital connectedness of family. Adoption speaks to our hearts, for what orphaned child would not want to be adopted by a loving, accepting father? Once again Packer writes,

> God will go out of his way to make his children feel his love for them, and know their privilege and security as members of his family. Adopted children need assurance that they belong, and a perfect parent will not withhold it.[15]

But as the verses imply, adoption must be "received." All men and women are orphaned from God until they receive the gift of salvation offered in Christ, the beloved Son of God who died on the cross to reconcile sinful people with a Holy Father.

This supernatural, parental commitment transcends even the bonds of our earthly parents' loyalty. As David wrote in Psalms, "Though my father and mother forsake me, the LORD will receive me" (Psalm 27:10).

GOD IS NOT THE FATHER OF ALL MEN

Some people believe that God is the Father of all. But this is not what the Bible teaches. The wealth of biblical doctrine teaches that God has a particular parental relationship with those who believe and put their faith in Him. The Gospel of John is clear: "He came to that which was his own, but his own did not receive him. Yet to all who received him, to those who believed in his name, he gave the right to become children of God" (John 1:11-12).

It is clear from Scripture that by believing and receiving Christ we become God's children, are adopted, and thus have God as our Father. Those who call God the "Father of all" often use the title and concept to express one or more of the following:

- ◆ God as the Creator.
- ◆ God as the Originator and Giver of all life.
- ◆ God as the Owner.
- ◆ God as each person's Father.

The title somewhat applies to the first three points. The Old Testament on occasion speaks of God our Father in the sense of being our Creator: "Is he not your Father, your Creator, who made you and formed you?" (Deuteronomy 32:6). And Paul speaks about God being "the Father, from whom all things came and for whom we live" (1 Corinthians 8:6). But in the few instances in which *Father* is used in the sense of creator and giver of life, the context is clear that the term is being used with such a connotation.

GOD IS THE FATHER OF ALL WHO BELIEVE

Scripture does not affirm that God is the Father of all men in the sense of a committed parental bond and relationship of Father to son. To teach so is to miss the whole impact of the gospel message of *becoming* a child of God through faith in the work of Jesus Christ on the cross. D. A. Carson writes, "The Gospel writers refer to God as Father only in contexts pertaining to the Messiah or to believers. He is not the Father of all men but the Father of Jesus and the Father of Jesus' disciples."[16]

Jesus went so far as to publicly denounce the Pharisees as not of God the Father because they did not believe Him. After they protested that "the only Father we have is God himself" (John 8:41), Jesus corrected them and said they had another "father." "You belong to your father, the devil, and you want to carry out your father's desire" (verse 44). Responsiveness to Jesus Christ in a loving relationship of trust is the indication of God being one's Father. As Jesus also said to those Pharisees, "If God were your Father, you would love me, for I came from God and now am here" (verse 42).

We are invited into a covenantal relationship with God as our Father—as the invitation reads in 2 Corinthians 6:17-18:

> Therefore come out from them and be separate, says the Lord. Touch no unclean thing, and I will receive you. I will be a Father to you, and you will be my sons and daughters, says the Lord Almighty.

God becomes the Father of the believer because of the substitutionary atonement of our Lord and Savior Jesus Christ. He enters into His covenant with the believer on the basis of the Cross. At this point of repentance and faith, the Holy Spirit confers sonship to the individual. Paul writes, "For you did not receive a spirit that makes you a slave again to fear, but you received the Spirit of sonship [*adoption*]. And by him we cry 'Abba, Father'" (Romans 8:15). In addition, Paul's phraseology in Galatians 4:7 presupposes that all men are *not* sons of God but rather become sons through faith and thus pass from the status of "slaves" to that of "sons." "So you are no longer a slave, but a son; and since you are a son, God has made you also an heir" (Galatians 4:7).

So essential is this recognition of God as our Father that it can be found in the greetings of seventeen of the twenty-one epistles and letters in the New Testament.[17]

Descriptively and functionally God is many things: He is the Creator, the Great Physician, the Good Shepherd, the Almighty, the Alpha and Omega, the Lord of hosts. Each designation carries specific absolute and relatable truths that encompass the attributes of God. But the most predominant and important role and title (besides that of "Lord") is the name and designation "Father." "In the N.T. the name 'Father' becomes the common name by which God is addressed. . . . This name is the highest revelation of God, God is not only the Creator, the Almighty One, the Faithful One, the King and Lord; He is also the Father of his people."[18] James I. Packer writes in *Knowing God,*

> You sum up the whole of New Testament teaching in a single phrase, if you speak of it as a revelation of the Fatherhood of the holy Creator. In the same way, you sum up the whole of New Testament religion if you describe it as the knowledge of God as one's holy Father.[19]

NO LONGER ORPHANS

The believer is more than just a follower, more than just a disciple, more than just a soldier in the Lord's army, more than just a pilgrim and sojourner, more than just a servant of God. Believers are sons and daughters: children of God their Father.

> If you want to know how well a person understands Christianity, find out how much he makes of the thought of being God's child, and having God as his Father. If this is not the thought that prompts and controls his worship and prayers and his whole out-look on life, it means that he does not understand Christianity very well at all. For everything that Christ taught, everything that makes the New Testament new, and better than the Old, everything that is dis-tinctively Christian as opposed to merely Jewish, is summed up in the knowledge of the Fatherhood of God. "Father" is the Christian name for God.[20]

I think of Sylvia Plath ending her life on this tragic note: "I never knew the love of a father." Of Marvin Gaye being killed by his father, and his friend revealing, "Marvin . . . never got the love from his father that he wanted." Of Saul Bellow's lament, "Everyone is born to be an orphan." Of Leo Tolstoy's longing for the warmth of motherly love, "My highest image of love . . . not cold, divine love." How many men and women have wound up dissatisfied because they looked to man to find what only God can truly give?

The believer need never go through life feeling like an emotional or spiritual orphan. Jesus' promise in John 14:18 stands today: "I will not leave you as orphans; I will come to you." And yet the glorious comfort this promise holds out so often eludes the children of God. In the next chapter we will explore the tragic ways in which poor earthly parenting can block our full enjoyment of the freedom we've been given to cry "Abba, Father."

FOUR

Parental Hangover

◆

*Yeah, he was around, but I definitely grew up without
a father. He sure didn't do any of the things that
Beaver Cleaver's father did. He was just a nice,
innocuous man. . . . He made no contribution
whatsoever to my growing up.*
"May"

◆

*He was the center of my world . . . and I never
doubted that I stood first in his heart.*
Eleanor Roosevelt
(long after the death of her father)

◆

*Though my father and mother forsake me,
the Lord will receive me.*
King David
Psalm 27:10

◆

I was talking to a middle-aged woman who grew up in an
"exemplary" Christian family. Her father, mother, brothers, and sisters all had served the Lord as a family while
they were growing up, and now they all were walking with
God as adults. As a child, she had been trained in Scripture. Her father led daily family devotions, and together the
family memorized large portions of Scripture. They sang
together as a family and performed in numerous churches.
As an adult, this woman was what we would call "solid" and
"mature." I thought that if anyone would have a healthy
view of God, she would.

That's why I was so surprised when in the midst of a
casual conversation about a sermon on God's love she said
to me, "I did not see much love from my dad. . . . He was

not very loving and affectionate. So I began to see God that way." How tragic, I thought, for a father to pass on to his child the knowledge of Scripture but not the knowledge of God as a loving Father. Even within Christian families it is possible to form an inaccurate image of God . . . even with people who have large portions of Scripture memorized. This woman's early perceptions of God were shaped by her negative impressions of her earthly father, and years later she still battled against those perceptions.

CARICATURES OF GOD

We often transfer to God caricatures we have of our fathers. So if we can identify and correct errors in our thinking about fathers, we will be better able to see God the Father more accurately. I am convicted that we need to be willing to nurture belief in the Bible's teaching of God's image, not in the distorted images we may have fashioned from childhood. I do not want to invite morbid introspection nor allow us too much room for blaming parents for our image of God. While we need to take stock in the baggage of our past, we should use it in a constructive way.

When we create a caricature of God, we sketch Him in cartoon-figure proportions, like the artists at a carnival or fair who exaggerate features to achieve comical likeness rather than accurate representation. Our caricatures of God are rarely humorous; in fact, they can be tragic, because we wind up distorting the holy image of a wondrous God. Yet it helps sometimes to laugh at ourselves, to see that our minds have funny ways of painting and distorting images. Like some late-night juvenile delinquent with a thick marker sketching moustaches, big ears, bushy eyebrows, and such on the bright billboard faces of subway advertisements, with big, broad strokes we can mar our image of God with theological vandalism.

At times in our lives, God challenges our erroneous thinking and the caricatures we have sketched of Him. One occasion has been a helpful reminder to me. It has been our family's habit to take summer vacations. One summer while in the midst of church planting we were in that stage of uncertain financial income. Early in the summer, I reluctantly figured we would not be able to go on a vacation. My line of thinking went like this: *Well, vacations aren't a necessity, so I shouldn't always expect to be able to go on one. But on the other hand, it would sure be nice to get away to the mountains for a week. I wonder if I should pray for a vacation. I guess I shouldn't, since vacations probably aren't that important to God.*

At this point I realized the picture I had painted of God. My mind has a funny way of reasoning, at times. Sometimes I find it is good to rattle on in my thinking so I can step back and listen to what I'm saying. My own thinking can convict me, as I point out to myself on occasion, "Do you realize what you are saying?" This time, I realized that I had a caricature of God as a "no-nonsense Father."

Where did I get my caricature of God as a no-nonsense Father? In general, I tended to view my parents' generation as a hard-working, no-nonsense generation. This was a good quality. They lived through the Depression and World War II and worked hard to build a future for themselves and the baby-boom generation. But I guess I created a caricature of fathers from this older generation. In the neighborhood where I grew up, the fathers (my father included) *worked* all the time, it seemed. They were always working: at their jobs, on their houses, on their lawns, or on their cars. I seldom remember seeing fathers *play* with their children. My dad was always trying to get me to do jobs with him around the house. There was always something to be fixed, cut, trimmed, oiled, nailed, painted, raked, or shoveled. And we didn't even live on a farm; we lived in the suburbs! And if I went off to play instead of helping Dad, boy, did I feel guilty. Fathers and sons worked on the house, on the lawn, on the car.

I never did learn how to work on cars very well. If my dad were alive he might say, "It's because you always wanted to go off and play that guitar, while I was out in the garage working on the car alone." The term *workaholic* had not been coined in the fifties and sixties, but the Protestant work ethic on which we put such a high premium in our country has been in full swing for a long time. That made it easy for me to conclude: work is important, leisure isn't. In my mind fathers worked hard; they didn't have much time to relax.

My inner thoughts about God really were,

God isn't interested in my vacation. He is a God of vision and essentials. God is a practical God. God answers prayers for significant needs and provisions. God isn't the kind of Father who would splurge on me. I don't think He would give me something just because I thought I wanted it.

There is both truth and error in those thoughts. I do believe God is practical, but does that mean He is predictable? God does not want to spoil us, but does that mean He is not, at times, overly generous? The promise of "abundant life" does not mean we will be given "materialistic abundant life" complete with big homes, nice cars, fat salaries, and great vacations. But does this mean that, at times, God won't give us unexpected and undeserved blessings?

Within a couple of days God shattered my personal caricature of Him as a no-nonsense Father who only gives practical and "necessary" gifts. I had settled in my heart that it was okay to not be able to take a vacation. And I honestly did not have a begrudging attitude toward God or the circumstances. But God wanted to expose an erroneous image I had of Him.

Within a couple of days, some friends at another church gave us a vacation gift: They made arrangements for us to stay at a cabin in the mountains. After receiving the news, I hung up the phone and was immediately convicted about my image of God. I realized I had put God in a box due to my image of Him. Now I sat back and affirmed: God is generous not stingy. God is not so practical that He cannot surprise us with unexpected gifts.

DADS WE HAVE KNOWN

If there is a connection between our perception of God and our images of our fathers, it is helpful then to take a look at these images. Let's take a few moments and explore the caricatures of fathers we have known and seen. For the sake of making a point, the following examples are deliberate caricatures.

The No-Nonsense Dad

This father was all business and little pleasure. He was the kind of dad who wouldn't put up with any back talk or laziness and always wanted his child to turn the stereo down. He was not much for small talk; he didn't have much to say, and when he did, it usually consisted of orders. Relaxing, recreation, and time off did not fit into his daily life.

The Forever-Practical Dad

This dad was utilitarian to a tee. Everything in life had to have a place, a purpose, and a function. This father would never give his child something unless it met a need, and even then the need had to be explicitly obvious. Both the no-nonsense dad and the forever-practical dad would never splurge or appear generous to their child. In reality, to the child, his dad's drive to be frugal appeared more like cheapness and stinginess.

The Nit-Picking Dad

This father was an inconsistent (or failed) perfectionist. Yet he was determined to make his child perfect. He was always explaining a better way, always correcting. He was never satisfied with the way his child performed, and he let the child know it. If something was not done exactly right, it was all wrong.

The Silent Dad

His child seldom knew what he was thinking. But mostly he figured it was disapproval. It wasn't just that Dad was quiet;

he appeared uninterested in communicating. He peered out from behind newspapers and magazines, and his child heard him muttering to himself amid the clinks and clattering of tools in the garage and basement.

The Absentee Dad
Similar to the silent dad, this dad was just never really around. Perhaps his work schedule kept him away, or perhaps he was gone due to divorce or abandonment. This father had no time or interest in being with his child.

The History-Teacher Dad
This dad had a lesson for every occasion. He always wanted his child to be in class. But most of the occasions for his lessons were the child's mistakes and failures. The child always knew Dad was going to give him a lecture.

The Drill-Sergeant Dad
This dad was quick to mete out discipline to any child who stepped out of line. This strict, regimented father didn't have children but boot-camp recruits. His primary role was discipline. Mom would always say, "Wait till your father gets home."

The Coach
This father was determined to live out all his missed opportunities for success through his child. So he drove and pushed and made plans for the child's achievements. Life became just that: wins-losses, game statistics, performance, measurements, and achievements. The child came to fear failure because it incurred Dad's disappointment.

The Angry Dad
This dad was always getting upset and angry, and his child always seemed to bear the brunt of it. Dad could be happy one moment and angry the next. This unpredictability kept the child uneasy. When would the next outburst come? The child lived in fear of the father.

The Pushover Dad

This Mr. Nice Guy would give whatever his child wanted. The child learned that with the right words at the right time he could get whatever he wanted. This was great for a time, but the child soon discovered that he didn't respect his father anymore.

The Dependent Dad

This father was more of a child than a father. He "needed" his child to support him, fulfill him, build him up, and ask little in return. Because of his own insecurity he relied too heavily on his child's involvement and was afraid for his child to grow up and leave him. This dad may have been a lot of fun sometimes, but eventually the child became the father or mother of the man.

The Martyr Dad

This father always felt unappreciated even after "all he's done for you." He needed constant affirmation to remind him how much he was needed and valued. He was an expert in laying on the guilt and kept his child tied to him by reminding him how much he "owed" his dad.

The Seductive Dad

This father tied his child to him through illegitimate and powerful sexual energy and/or abuse. This pathetic father may have trained his innocent child to perform secret sexual "favors" or to function as a "surrogate spouse" who is required to meet adult emotional needs. He destroyed both his child's soul and his own to get his needs met. The child eventually learned that a very sacred trust between father and child has been violated.

The Passive (or Cowardly) Dad

This father had no backbone and no nerve. By his lack of action he proved he was uncaring and unprotecting. He stood by indifferently while his child was hurt or in need. He did not stand up for the child against a domineering wife or other harmful authority figures. He seemed too concerned with his own self-preservation or personal agenda to put himself on the line for his needy child.

THE CONNECTION

These are just a few *caricatures* of fathers and how their fathering can be perceived by the child. The point is that many of us have specific images, however distorted, of fathers. When we come into our relationship with God we often transfer these images to God. J. B. Phillips stated, "The early conception of God is almost invariably founded upon the child's idea of his father."[1]

Though there is not a necessary correlation between one's earthly father and one's subsequent image of God, there is, however, a significant correlation between the two images. Many counselors attest to the intermingling of these father images. Dr. Paul D. Meier, a Christian counselor and author, observes,

> Patients who had cold, passive, and frequently absent fathers tend to believe that God is some cold, indifferent being out in space somewhere. . . . Patients who had rigid, demanding, negativistic, overly punitive fathers have tended to fall into two categories: some of these patients hated their fathers so much that they became atheists as an unconscious rebellion against the existence of their fathers; on the other hand, most of them believe there is a God, but that God is a mean old man up there, holding a whip and just daring us to break one of his rules so he can snap us with it![2]

For the sake of broad generalization, images tend to be either overly authoritative or overly permissive. Of those who had demanding, punitive earthly fathers, Meier points out,

> These are the Christians who tend to migrate to legalistic, negativistic churches, where it will be easier for

them to live up to their unrealistic concept of God's standards, based upon the standards of their earthly fathers. These patients wanted their earthly fathers to accept them, so they became rigidly perfectionistic in order to win their father's approval, which they seldom won anyway.[3]

These people, in turn, base their acceptance from God upon their performance and rigid behavioral standards. Sadly, they fear God's punishment, and many of them never really feel forgiven by God. At the other end of the spectrum are those who had permissive, lenient fathers. Meier writes,

I have also had a group of patients whose fathers were the overly sweet type, who pampered them, bought them whatever they pointed at in stores, seldom contradicted them, and hardly ever punished them. These people tend to be religious liberals who are quite idealistic, deny the sinful nature of man, and pretend there is no literal hell.[4]

Vague notions of God tend to make us want to create God in the image of a big, warm-hearted friend. C. S. Lewis remarked,

What would really satisfy us would be a God who said of anything we happened to like doing, "What does it matter so long as they are contented?" We want, in fact, not so much a Father in heaven as a grandfather in heaven—a senile benevolence who, as they say, "liked to see young people enjoying themselves," and whose plan for the universe was simply that it might be truly said at the end of each day, "a good time was had by all."

   Not many people, I admit, would formulate a theology in precisely those terms: but a conception not very different lurks at the back of many minds.[5]

PARENTAL HANGOVER

I like the term J. B. Phillips used to refer to erroneous images of fathers that linger on and distort our image of God. He called it "parental hangover."[6]

How can the particular caricatures of dads described earlier distort our image of the heavenly Father? What kind of "hangover" effect can they have if we see God as being like them?

God as the No-Nonsense Father

I may have difficulty relaxing in my relationship with Him. I may see Him as only interested in me in terms of how I can contribute to helping Him fulfill His goals. My relationship with God may become all business.

God as the Forever-Practical Father

I may consider Him uninterested in my personal interests unless they are "basic needs." I may see Him as unsympathetic to inner, emotional needs because practical people are mostly concerned with external tangibles. I may find it difficult to see Him interested in being generous or attentive to me personally.

God as the Nit-Picking Father

I will see Him as one who is never satisfied with me. The burden of living under the scrutinizing gaze of a perfectionist God will cause me to become legalistic. I will always try to earn God's favor, yet never feel that I measure up. I will eventually grow weary of His demanding dissatisfaction.

God as the History-Teacher Father

I will grow weary of always being in the classroom instead of at home. Learning lessons and being a teachable student are essential to Christian growth, but Christianity isn't just being in a classroom twenty-four hours a day. If we believe God is only interested in teaching us lessons, we will find ourselves yearning for a Father rather than a professor.

God as the Drill-Sergeant Father

I will find I am always anticipating punishment. My motive for keeping in line will not be love but the fear of incurring God's wrath. When I mess up I will cringe in fearful expectation of punishment. I will misinterpret life events, misfortunes, and accidents as God's disciplinary and punitive paybacks for my offenses.

God as the Silent or Absentee Father

I will feel alone in the Christian life. I will perceive God as being "up there" and myself "down here." I will not understand the ministry of the indwelling Holy Spirit nor the concept of Emmanuel, "God with us." I will not see God as interested in relating to me as a person whom He really *sees* and values.

God as the Coach

I will conclude that He really isn't interested in me as His son. I will think He is interested only in my potential, my performance. I will see my usefulness in terms of achievement and wins and losses. I may fear that He will "kick me off the team." Eventually, I may even begin to see Him as involved with the "first string players," not noticing me as a "second string player."

God as the Angry Father

I will find it difficult to relax around Him. I will live in nervous dread wondering when the ax will fall. I will see Him as seldom pleased, as I wait for His silence to turn to impatience. I will see God as capricious, inconsistent, and uncontrolled. He will become to me a God who takes me out behind the woodshed to inflict a serious beating for each offense. I will tiptoe around neurotically trying to appease Him, or else in frustration I will walk away from Him in a huff, venting my anger at Him and others around me.

God as the Pushover Dad

I will push and manipulate to see what I can get and what I can get away with. Children usually wind up without respect for a pushover father. I will think that I am in control of the relationship and even God. When reality proves *me* wrong, I may wonder what's wrong with *God*. I will also wind up seeing God as a little God, with little power. I will wind up with a Caspar Milquetoast God.

God as the Dependent Dad
I may conclude that He "needs" me (people) in order to be fulfilled. I may perceive Him as having been lonely and in need of company when He made man, and I may think that without people God wouldn't know what to do. I may fear being "swallowed up" by a God who wants *all* of me for Himself so He will be fulfilled and glorified.

God as the Martyr Dad
I may think that He expects my faithful obedience and service as a payback for all that I owe Him. I may imagine that God laments, "After all I've done for you, this is how you treat Me? This is the thanks I get?" I may mistakenly think that Christ died on the cross in order to tie me to Himself in guilty appreciation for His great sacrifice for me. I may misinterpret Paul's words, "You are not your own; you were bought at a price" (1 Corinthians 6:19-20), as a burdensome contract that robs me of liberty and joy.

God as the Seductive Dad
I may not trust His schooling because I fear His hidden agenda. I may shudder at the concept of being "used" by God for fear of being *mis*used. I may fear rather than rely on His power, and I may find it impossible to trust that He has my best interest foremost on His mind.

God as the Passive Dad
I will see Him as weak, undependable, and indifferent. I will not see Him as a protector but as one who passively stands by while I am hurt and endangered. I will not naturally turn to Him for refuge, but rather I will be compelled to protect myself and to take matters into my own hands.

Whenever trials come I will not see them as designed by a wise, powerful Father, but instead I will conclude (as one recent bestseller did) that God may be nice enough, but He isn't all-powerful.

NO LONGER VICTIMS

Floyd McClung, Jr., recounts a revealing incident in his book *The Father Heart of God.* A friend of his, fresh out of theological studies, told a hardened, streetwise teenager that God was like a father. The young man's eyes glared with hatred as he said, "If he's anything like my old man, you can have him!" This man had good reason for his anger: his father had raped his sister repeatedly and beaten his mother regularly.[7]

Unfortunately, this young man's response is more commonplace than we may care to think. But we need to be careful that we don't blame our parents for our opinion of God. Although it is natural to project the images we have of our parents onto our heavenly Father, we can draw hope from the fact that God is a restorer. He wants to draw our sight far above the imperfections of our earthly parents to the beauty of His own face.

THE BALANCED PARENTING OF GOD

Although I am focusing in this chapter on the impact our father may have had on our concept of God, our mother may have had a great influence as well. This can be especially true in families where the father was absent and the mother was the only parental influence the children knew.

Fortunately, God Himself is a perfectly complete and "balanced" parent, in that He has both maternal and paternal qualities. Whether our greatest deficits in earthly parenting came from our father or our mother, God can overcome both because He is both strong and tender.

Though God is a "Father," His compassion and tenderness are described in both fatherly and motherly images:

As a father has compassion on his children,
    so the LORD has compassion on those who fear
        him. (Psalm 103:13)

As a mother comforts her child,
    so will I comfort you. (Isaiah 66:13)

When God describes the depth of His bond to His people, He draws on the image of a mother and child:

Can a mother forget the baby at her breast
    and have no compassion on the child she has
        borne? (Isaiah 49:15)

Scripture never addresses God as "our mother," and any notion of that being a theological necessity would be out of keeping with biblical theology. But the wealth of imagery of the Fatherhood of God relies upon both the paternal and maternal instincts of God as a parent. As Oswald Chambers wrote, "The mothering affection of God is revealed all through the Old Testament."[8]

We need strong, biblical images of our glorious, majestic, powerful, incomparable God. We rob God of His greatness and glory and rob ourselves of a healthy relationship with a loving Father when we limit God by our "parental hangovers."

It is only when we limit the mind's stirrings after its Maker by imposing upon it half-forgotten images of our own earthly parents, that we grow frustrated in spirit and wonder why for us the springs of worship and love do not flow. We must leave behind "parental hangover" if we are to find a "big enough" God.[9]

The primary image of the Christian's relationship with God the Father is not the classroom, not the woodshed, not the family business, not the military boot camp, not the football field (nor showers or the bench). God desires a

Father-child relationship: a relationship between a perfect, loving Father and His beloved child.

I was talking to an attractive young mother who appeared quite confident and comfortable around others. Her countenance and vibrant spirit surprised me all the more once I knew her story. While she spoke I tried not to appear shocked, but inside I alternated between sadness and anger. Her story also made me praise God for the miracle of restored lives. She has given me permission to use a portion of her testimony here:

> I can't really explain it, but I have always been dominated by the men in my life. There was incest in my family . . . things that I have told only a couple of people. I am not a passive person. But somehow I allowed this to happen to me. As a child, though, you don't always know what to do . . . you are depending upon Mom and Dad to help. Sometimes the damage has already been done before you figure out that Mom or Dad are the ones who really need help. I am finally trying to deal with my past. I have decided to go to my father and tell him it was wrong what he did to me. I'm terrified, but I believe God wants me to do this. Maybe he'll be convicted and apologize. Who knows? I am not angry or bitter toward my father. I've forgiven him, and I love him. But I feel sorry for him. I am thankful that God loves and accepts me and has made me a new creation.

You may have been a victim, but you do not need to go on victimizing yourself with the past. Through the inner redemptive power of God, through *choosing* to believe the image of God presented in Scripture, and through the affirmation and acceptance of healthy substitute families of believers, this woman was able, over time, to know and trust God as her loving Father.

We may have had a traumatic experience that has hindered a healthy image of God, but it need not be an excuse to avoid restoring our Father's image. We do not have to be helpless victims of parental hangover in our relationship with the Parent who loves us perfectly.

I have found that one of the most important applications in the Christian life tends to be forgotten . . . *believing*. I don't mean having enough faith, I mean believing what the Scriptures say about who God is and what He is like. People usually want to know what they can *do*, and many of us take a passive approach to *believing* truth. Because of our experience, memories, or doubts we sometimes say, "I just can't believe that," or "I have a hard time believing God on that point." Then we somehow expect faith to push away those doubts over the course of time. Healthy doubts are fine. But remember the man who said to Jesus, "I do believe; help me overcome my unbelief" (Mark 9:24).

One of the most important parts of having a good image of God as our Father is to believe the truth of Scripture. We must let the truth of Scripture transform our minds from within (Romans 12:2). The transformation process begins by making a choice to believe what Scripture says about who God is and then allow Scripture to inform our inner voice rather than our own ideas or negative experiences.

PART II

Learning to See God as He Is

FIVE

A Father with His Heart on His Sleeve

My father and I were always on the most distant terms when I was a boy — sort of armed neutrality, so to speak.
Mark Twain

"But while he was still a long way off, his father saw him and was filled with compassion for him; he ran to his son, threw his arms around him and kissed him."
Jesus Christ
Luke 15:20

"My heart is changed within me; all my compassion is aroused."
The Lord
Hosea 11:8

One day one of my eight-year-old sons was in the living room playing while I was reading. He had a wooden yardstick, and he was holding it and jumping over it. I heard the crack but pretended that I didn't in order to see his response. Immediately after the sound of the crack, he scurried out of the room. He stopped in the hall, just out of my sight, so he could survey the extent of the damage and figure out his next move.

God knows the hearts of His children. He knows we sin and make mistakes. He knows when to discipline sternly and when to be gentle. He knows that sometimes we run from Him and compound our problems. He knows when our hearts and spirits are heavy because of inner conviction and fear. He knows when it is time to lift us up. But at the heart of it all is God's desire for a loving, meaningful relationship with each of His children.

As my son waited in the hall, I smiled and thought, *It's pretty hard to get away with something when Dad is right there in the room.* So I calmly called him back into the room and asked, "What happened?"

He said, "I don't know." (All children seem to say "I don't know" when they are stalling for time.)

Then I said softly but matter-of-factly, "You cracked the yardstick, didn't you?"

He was caught between owning up to it and wanting to hide the evidence. So he said, "No, it's. . . ." His voice trailed off as he held up the two pieces and tried to see if he could fit them together at the splintered break. So I helped out again and asked, "It's broken, isn't it?" I spoke softly each time, because I knew this was a teachable moment.

I could see he was disappointed with himself. I knew that my son did not like disappointing me; he wanted to please his dad. The sadness made him take in a deep breath, and his whole countenance and spirit drooped as he slowly sighed. We both knew he was sorry for breaking the stick, but perhaps he was more sorry for running away, covering it up, and thinking of denying it all. As his father, in my heart I knew my son had a tender heart. He wasn't some mischievous little boy whose heart is only good when caught.

I also knew that once again God was giving me a window into my relationship with Him. I couldn't help seeing myself in my son: a small boy caught before God my Father with a mixed bag of guilt and regret, the evidence in my hands. Just like my son, I seem to have the knack for doing the dumb thing when God is right there in the room. I can't fool God, and I can't run from Him. And I know better when I try.

I told my son that he didn't need to hide from me. I explained that I was more upset that he tried to hide and deny what he did than I was about the yardstick being broken. Seeing that he was truly convicted, I decided I did not need to discipline him; his own heart was disciplining him. The incident became an opportunity to teach and encourage.

I went over to him and we sat down. I put my arm around him, and we looked at the yardstick. I smiled as I thought to myself, *I won't tell him it cost only thirty-nine cents*, because the yardstick isn't really the issue, our relationship is. Besides, he only broke off the last ten inches of it. I told him it was okay, now we would have just a two-foot stick.

God the Father is compassionate. He knows our guilt, our fear of punishment, and our disappointment in ourselves, as well as our penchant for sometimes minimizing or justifying our sins. He desires an openness that causes us to seek Him and not hide from Him. He knows when we fall and He desires to help us own up to it all in moments of crestfallen humility. He knows the sorrow of our deep sighs, and He steps in and pumps life and hope into us.

Do you see God as a Father who desires to know and relate to you? Or do you see Him as a distant, demanding Deity, more concerned with your performance than your friendship?

GOD'S ATTITUDE TOWARD HIS CHILDREN

It would have been a thrill to watch the interaction between Jesus and the children who came around Him. He must have had a warm, smiling look on His face and a playful gleam in His eyes that made children feel free to approach Him and climb up into His lap, even tug on His beard. The gospels never tell us that Jesus smiled, but the best evidence of His friendly and smiling countenance is the fact that children gathered around Him. Jesus enjoyed children, and they could see that. He was approachable then, and He is approachable now.

Children are quick to pick up whether an adult likes them or not. They can see it in an adult's eyes and countenance. Children quickly apprehend their father's attitude toward them, and this attitude makes an impression on them as much as anything their father says. The best parents clearly enjoy their children. You can observe it when you are with them, and you can hear it when they talk about them.

I remember being at a church cookout and playing in the pool with a few five-to-nine-year-old children. We were playing some silly game I had made up in which the kids got to dunk my head under the water. We laughed and had a great time. Later, one of the elders told me that his seven-year-old daughter had a memorable time and thought it was the greatest thing in the world that she got to dunk "Pastor Phil's" head under the water. I had become someone that she felt closer to as a child. She probably remembered nothing about my sermons, but I was a "real person" to her.

God our Father wants to become a real person to us, Someone who is more than just the moral Judge and Ruler of the universe. He wants us to sense His approachability and His accepting smile. Christianity is more than just a "theological relationship." It is a personal, intimate relationship. God does not look at us merely as recipients of the theological transactions of substitutionary atonement. God's love is personal.

FREE FROM FEAR TO RELATE IN PEACE

Because God has made believers His children, we have a privileged relationship with the Father. As Paul wrote in Romans 8:15, "For you did not receive a spirit that makes you a slave again to fear, but you received the Spirit of sonship. And by him we cry, 'Abba, Father.'" Our salvation has significant bearing not only on our eternal destiny but also on the nature of our daily relationship with God. We have entered into a relationship in which we do not need to labor in slavery and cower in fear before God.

What does it mean to be a "slave again to fear"? Paul is referring to our past status before God, when we were anxious and fearful about God's disposition. Before accepting Christ, we were slaves to fear because our status depended—at least we thought so—on our performance and righteousness. We were also in fear of death. The writer of Hebrews speaks of Christ freeing us "who all our lives were held in slavery by their fear of death" (2:15). The basis of our relationship with the Father is the work of Christ accomplished on the cross. The "spirit of sonship" makes it possible for us to relate to God in a relationship in which we can confidently call God "Father."

The following chart demonstrates how our status changes when we become believers. Our relationship to God changes from "enemies" and "children of wrath" to "sons" and "adopted" children with "full rights."

BEFORE SALVATION	AFTER TRUSTING CHRIST
Previously Designated	*Reconciled Status*
a. "Enemies" (Romans 5:8-11).	a. "Sons" or "children" (John 1:12, Galatians 4:7, 1 John 3:1).
b. "Slaves" (Galatians 4:1-8) who *"did not know God."*	b. *"Adopted" children* call Him "Abba" with "full rights" (Romans 8:15-17, Galatians 4:5-7).
c. "Children of wrath" (Ephesians 2:3, NASB).	c. "Children of light" (John 12:36, Ephesians 5:8).
d. "Foreigners and aliens" (Ephesians 2:19).	d. "Members of God's household" (Ephesians 2:19).
e. "Sons of disobedience" (Ephesians 2:2, NASB).	e. "Sons and daughters" of the Father (2 Corinthians 6:18).

The great message of the gospel is not simply that we have escaped death and hell, but that we are no longer enemies of God, no longer aliens: we are sons and daughters of the Most High God. God has accepted and entered into a loving relationship with each of us. Because of Christ "we have been justified though faith" and "we have peace with God through our Lord Jesus Christ, through whom we have *gained access* by faith into this *grace in which we now stand*" (Romans 5:1-2, emphasis added). The believer stands in a relationship of grace and peace in which Christ is our faithful High Priest, able to "sympathize with our weaknesses" (Hebrews 4:15). In this relationship we are urged to approach God the Father confidently: "Let us then approach the throne of grace with confidence, so that we may receive mercy and find grace to help us in our time of need" (4:16). The writer of Hebrews gives us a double assurance: Jesus is "not ashamed to call them brothers" (2:11); and "God is not ashamed to be called their God" (11:16).

A SPECIAL ENDEARMENT

When Paul tells us we can address God as "Abba, Father," he is indicating that the believer is on special terms with his Father. *Abba* is an endearing term borrowed from Aramaic. It refers only to God in the New Testament, three times (Mark 14:36, Romans 8:15, Galatians 4:6). The word *abba* is derived from baby language. It would be taught to infants being weaned from their mothers. The babies would learn to say *'abba* (meaning "daddy") and *'imma* (meaning "mommy"). Eventually the word *abba* became a common form of addressing one's father, no longer restricted to children. *Abba* was not a flippant term, but a term that signaled an emotional connection. It combined both the personable intimacy of "daddy" with the warm respect of "father." It "acquired the warm familiar ring which we may feel in such an expression as 'dear father.'"[1]

Jesus originally used the term *Abba, Father* when He addressed God the Father in Gethsemane (Mark 14:36). This was an original concept, which had not been used in Jewish literature up to that point. In fact, the Jews felt uncomfortable calling God their Father. But in his epistles to the Romans and Galatians, Paul tells believers that we may address God with the same personal and endearing term that Jesus used. We may call Him "Daddy," "dear Father," "Dad."

This term is not to lead to a disrespectful, casual,

"buddy-buddy" or flippant approach to God. But it is meant to signal His approachability.

GOD DELIGHTS IN HIS CHILDREN

In speaking of God disciplining us as a Father does a child, Proverbs says God's motivation is love and a Father's delight in His son (Proverbs 3:12). In Psalm 18, David writes that God delivered him simply because God "delighted in me" (verse 19).

On one particularly gloomy and skeptical day, I remember thinking that God only loves me because He has to, because Christ died for me, and because I put my trust in Him. I thought, *He doesn't really like me or love me. He is obligated to love me.* I was working through the implications of God's personal love for me. The remarkable truth is that God the Father does love each of us. He likes us because He chooses to do so. It is important for the believer to realize that God has a favorable attitude toward His children. I have chosen to use the word *attitude* because God is a Being with a personality.

Have you ever seen a parent singing to a child to comfort and quiet the infant? Parents have always sung lullabies to their babies. The language of Zephaniah 3:17 recalls this sort of parent-child imagery: "He will take great delight in you, he will quiet you with his love, he will rejoice over you with singing." This imagery reminds us of a parent comforting a child. The first phrase literally reads, "He will delight in you with joy." The word *delight* also means "rejoice." Similarly, the psalmist declares, "For the LORD takes delight in his people; he crowns the humble with salvation. Let the saints rejoice in this honor" (Psalm 149:4-5).

Though God takes delight in our obedience, and though He can be displeased by our actions and attitudes, we must realize that His overall attitude toward His children is positive. God takes "delight" in His people simply because they are His. He delights in us, and He cherishes us. Psalm 17:14 says of God, "You still the hunger of those you cherish."

The word *cherish* indicates that God treasures us because we are dear to Him. Did you know that God cherishes you personally? What an honor to be cherished by God Almighty.

GOD PITIES HIS CHILDREN

Sometimes as a parent you look at your children (whether they are three months, three years, thirteen, or thirty-three years old) and your heart goes out to them. Sometimes your heart breaks for them. God our Father goes through the same thing:

> As a father has compassion on his children,
>> so the LORD has compassion on those who
>>> fear him;
> for he knows how we are formed,
>> he remembers that we are dust.
>>> (Psalm 103:13-14)

God knows our frailty, our humanness. He realizes that He is infinitely holy and consuming, while His children are finite and easily consumed. The *King James Version* uses the term *pity*: "As a father pitieth his children, so the LORD pitieth them that fear him."

The root of the Hebrew word here refers to deep love, mercy, and compassion. Isaiah uses this same word to refer to a mother's love for a nursing baby (49:15). A close derivative of this word actually means "womb." The word used in Psalm 103:13, then, encompasses ideas of tenderness and deep feeling for someone who is needy.

God who is the judge, jury, and executioner of all unredeemed mankind has a soft spot in His heart for His children. And in the right sense, at times He is a pushover for His children.

In His anger and judgment He pronounces sentence. But even in that He realizes His love, tenderness, and covenant. As with Israel in Hosea:

"How can I give you up, Ephraim?
How can I hand you over, Israel?
How can I treat you like Admah?
How can I make you like Zeboiim?
My heart is changed within me;
all my compassion is aroused."
(Hosea 11:8)

The word *aroused* literally means to "grow warm." In Scripture it is used in the sense of being deeply moved—of the compassion of family members toward each other.

The concept of God's pity is also linked to His condescension. Christ's coming to earth was God's visible act of condescension in which He literally and voluntarily descended and came down to our level. God graciously did something regarded as beneath His dignity. . . . He took on human flesh and became a servant (Philippians 2:6-8). God's condescension is His readiness to view us as we are—"he remembers that we are dust" (Psalm 103:13-14)—and yet still show kindness.

In Psalm 18 we have an image of God coming down as a Great Rescuer from Heaven to help man in need. Verse 9 says, "He parted the heavens and came down." The psalmist describes God's power and might, but the tenderness and sympathy come through in this image: "You stoop down to make me great" (Psalm 18:35).

The *New American Standard Bible* translates the verse, "Thy gentleness [or condescension] makes me great." The word gives us the sense of God, the Mighty One who is far superior to man, descending, bending over, stooping down to make His child great.

How many times have you seen fathers and mothers stoop down to help their child? A parent stoops down to give good eye contact and listen attentively. A parent gets down at a child's level so that the child knows his parent is interested and involved and so the parent's size is less intimidating. That's a picture of our God—of our Father. He *stoops down* to make us great, to lift us up.

GOD'S HEART GOES OUT TO HIS CHILDREN

Do you see God as a Father who is emotionally involved with His children? Scripture says that we can "grieve" the Holy Spirit (Isaiah 63:10, Ephesians 4:30). God's love for us is such that not only can all His compassions be aroused but His heart can be grieved, saddened, and hurt by us. When Scripture records, "In all their distress he too was distressed," we are given a glimpse into the heart of God (Isaiah 63:9). God's heart is such that He hurts and aches along with His people.

I remember my first year as a new father. One night while holding my child I realized how much I loved the little infant. But I asked myself, *Why? Why should I love my child? He hasn't done anything to earn my love. All he does is eat, sleep, cry, and make dirty diapers. He can't mow the lawn, take out the trash, or clean his room. He can't even talk, let alone carry on a conversation. So why do I love my child so much?*

As I thought this through, I realized that I loved my child because he was *my child*. He didn't have to do anything to make me love him; I loved him unconditionally. Is God's love for us any less? Scripture says, "This is love: not that we loved God, but that he loved us and sent his Son as an atoning sacrifice for our sins. . . . We love because he first loved us" (1 John 4:10,19).

The Hebrew word *hesed* is a rich term that is difficult to translate into English. *Hesed* is the loyal love of God, the committed, covenantal bond God established with His children. The love of God is best understood in terms of a committed relationship.

When you look at the love of God, put aside works, discipleship, obedience, service, and anything else you may mistakenly suppose earns you God's love. Each of those have their place in your relationship with God, but they do not secure for you the love of God. Jesus assures His followers of the depth of God's love with these profound words: "As the Father has loved me, so have I loved you" (John 15:9).

There is no greater unconditional love in the universe than God's love for Jesus Christ. Jesus compares His love for us to the divine love of the Holy Trinity. When praying to the Father in John 17, Jesus once again compares God's love for the believer with the divine love inherent in the Trinity: "You . . . have loved them even as you have loved me" (verse 23).

God the Father loves us with the same love He has for Christ. This is a committed love, a secure love, a perfect love. This is not to say that obedience, discipleship, and service are not significant aspects of responding to and walking with God. Our Lord loves us unconditionally, yet as in all vital relationships, love must be reciprocal. To experience the benefits of God's relational love the believer needs to participate in the conditions of the relationship. But let us not diminish the glory of God's love by placing the burden back on the believer to keep it and earn it. As J. I. Packer said,

> God will go out of his way to make his children feel his love for them, and know their privilege and security as members of his family. Adopted children need assurance that they belong, and a perfect parent will not withhold it.[2]

A small article caught my eye one day as I was flipping through the newspaper. It was about a father's devotion to his son. A disabling bike accident prevented the young man from attending college regularly, so for thirteen years this father had gone to classes to take notes for his disabled son so that he could graduate from college.

The son's therapist said, "I've never seen such devotion." But the father's words seemed to say it all: "As a parent, you love your children, *nothing is a sacrifice* if you love them."[3] I stared at the picture of the proud father with his broad, toothy smile, standing next to his son who was dressed in a graduation cap and gown. I was astounded by the father's devotion. For a moment I was jealous.

Then I remembered the words *how much more*. I wondered, *Does God love me that much?* Is God's devotion to His children any less astounding? "If you, then, though you are evil, know how to give good gifts to your children, *how much more* will your Father in heaven give good gifts to those who ask him!" (Matthew 7:11, emphasis added).

Jesus is not speaking about men being "evil" parents in the sense of villainous or cruel. He is saying that even imperfect, selfish, sinful men are motivated to be generous, decent, good fathers. If sinful men are capable of being good fathers, is not God our heavenly Father also motivated and capable? "How much more" wonderful is God than even the best of human fathers?

We need to see God's deep-felt emotion for us. Sometimes great human examples of love help us put His love into perspective. There is one such moving scene in the famous play *A Raisin in the Sun* by Lorraine Hansberry.

In the play Walter Lee Younger has a dream to make a better life for his poor, black, Chicago family. But he needs the insurance money his mother just received from his father's death in order to make a business investment. Reluctant at first, his mama finally agrees to give him a large portion of it. But the dream is shattered before it ever begins when Walter's "business partner" skips town with all the money. We shake our heads at Walter for his lack of foresight and his foolishness. Like the prodigal son, Walter is a beaten man who has lost his family's inheritance.

His sister is ready to disown him, with good reason. Walter also lost her portion of the insurance money that she was planning to use to go to college. "He's no brother of mine," she says to her mother. Then in a powerful and emotional outburst, Walter's mother expresses the depth of her parental love.

MAMA: You done wrote his epitaph too—like the rest of the world? Well, who give you the privilege? . . . I thought I taught you to love him.

BENEATHA: Love him? There is nothing left to love.

MAMA: There is always something left to love. And if you ain't learned that, you ain't learned nothing. Have you cried for that boy today? I don't mean for yourself and for the family 'cause we lost the money. I mean for him: what he been through and what it done to him. *Child, when do you think is the time to love somebody the most? When they done good and made things easy for everybody? Well, then you ain't through learning—because that ain't the time at all. It's when he's at his lowest and can't believe in hisself 'cause the world done whipped him so! When you starts measuring somebody, measure him right, child, measure him right. Make sure you done taken into account what hills and valleys he come through before he got to wherever he is.*[4]

That is the heart of a parent! It is a moment in the play that brings tears to your eyes. It makes you want to stand and cheer, "Yes, that's what a parent's love is! And God's love is greater!"

The wonder of human love is exceeded by divine love. I'm afraid in our desire to preserve God's divinity we sometimes drain Him of His passion and make Him too unemotional. God is a passionate God! He feels deeply and is vitally attached to His children. We need to have an image of Him that moves us to tears and cheers.

The tragedy for many Christians is that sometimes we do not connect with the real heart of God. We tend to come to the story of the prodigal son with a ho-hum attitude. We've heard it before, and it seems old. But we need to read it with a new heart, we need to charge it full of emotion, we need to be amazed by the father's love because it is a picture of our heavenly Father's love.

The story of the prodigal son should more aptly be entitled, "The Parable of the Loving Father." I am sure this father was hurt by his son leaving home, especially under the circumstances. The son was leaving home to indulge his own wild desires. In his way, the prodigal son was as foolish as Walter Lee.

The son finally came to his senses. Knowing his father's kindness, he decided to return home. His mind must have been full of ways to make it all up to his dad. Along the trail home, I suspect that the son was rehearsing his opening lines for that all-important moment when he would finally face his father.

The father probably scanned the horizon daily, straining his eyes to spot a particular solitary silhouette coming across the heat waves rising from the arid land. And perhaps on more than one occasion, upon catching a shadowy figure, he leaned forward and squinted his eyes to make out who it was. In the tension of the moment his heart might have beat a bit faster in anticipation—only to realize it wasn't his son but one of the field hands or a stranger.

One day the father saw a figure in the distance, as he had many times before. Perhaps he caught a glimpse of something while talking to one of the servants, or perhaps while walking to the house he stopped to wipe the sweat from his brow and glanced in the direction his son had taken. And seeing a figure a long way off he stopped wiping his brow and slowly took a step forward, squinting into the distance. And with the second step his heart beat faster. As only a parent can, he recognized his son's particular walk and stature.

Tense with hope, the father took a quick step or two and broke into a run, not taking his eyes off his son for fear it might be an illusion. He called a couple of servants to fall in behind him. He already knew his plan, for he thought often of this moment. And he ran. It had been a long time since he had run this hard, but he hardly gave it a thought as his sandals flapped up clumps of dirt, and dust clung to his disheveled robe.

By the time the son realized the man running toward him was his father, he might have frozen in his tracks wondering if his father was enraged and would drive him off.

But as he saw the bright eyes and toothy grin, he must have momentarily forgotten his rehearsed lines.

A lesser parent would have waited for the son to arrive. He would have held back and expected his son to come and find him in the barn or the field. A lesser father would have appeared a bit stoic and unmoved. He would have perhaps not even lifted his eyes to meet the son, but instead would have shown his disapproval and hurt.

A lesser father would have outlined the conditions of the son's return instead of laying out the red carpet unconditionally. He would have waited for an apology before showing acceptance, and may have not warmed up until his son showed some real signs of change. A lesser father would have made it clear that the son had to prove himself worthy again.

A lesser father would have wanted some explanations: "Where did all the money go?" "Why did you act so foolishly?" A lesser father would have given a speech instead of a party. He would have given the son a red-faced stare instead of the red robe of honor and made the son feel guilty instead of special.

But in the parable in Luke 15 we are not dealing with an average father. "While he was still a long way off, his father saw him and was filled with compassion for him; he ran to his son, threw his arms around him and kissed him" (verse 20).

In his exuberance, the father may have nearly knocked his son over as he came bowling into him and embraced him with a bear hug. This father was not hesitant or uncomfortable showing his affection. Perhaps in tears of joy, he simply uttered words full of emotion, "My son, my son." How the meaning of sonship must have burst upon that young man's heart as his father dispensed with all the explanations and rehearsed lines of apology and quickly proceeded to throw a party in honor of his son's return. This was a time to rejoice. This was a time for love and acceptance and forgiveness to take center stage.

Our Father in Heaven takes equal delight in us, His

wayward children. Our Father in Heaven is no less compassionate than the prodigal son's father. Our Father's heart goes out to us. Like the prodigal's father, our Father wears His heart on His sleeve.

I remember the times when I felt more like the prodigal's brother. I would think back to when I was saved, when the angels rejoiced, and Heaven had a party in my honor . . . "a son was lost and now is found!" After walking with God for some time, however, I have at times wondered if He isn't disappointed with me. Perhaps I haven't lived up to His expectations. Sometimes I have caught myself wondering, as the prodigal's brother did, if my Father would still throw a party for me. But the father in the story assured the brother that his place was secure. I am reminded of Lamentations 3:22: "His compassions never fail."

Do you feel refreshed and secure in the love of God? Or perhaps the focus of your relationship with God has become how well you perform. Perhaps you have walked with God awhile. Maybe you've slipped and stumbled and plodded along. Maybe you wonder if God and the angels would still throw a joyful party in your honor. The prodigal's brother had been performing but lost sight of the relationship. He said in anger to his father, "Look! All these years I've been slaving for you and never disobeyed your orders" (Luke 15:29). Many believers are like that. We have been faithful Christians, but our heart attitude lost something and it all became "slaving." The father assured his son, as God does His children, "My son . . . you are always with me" (15:31). However, while we are always with Him, we may not always feel close to Him. Getting wrapped up in our "slaving" often leads to drudgery and doubt. We need to remember that even when we have lost our perspective, God has not: "His compassions never fail. They are new every morning; great is your faithfulness" (Lamentations 3:22-23).

SIX

Father Knows Best

The making of a man, even when the raw
material was as pliable as I, often seemed
brutally hard without the help of a father
to handle the rough passages.
Russell Baker
Growing Up

I will instruct you (says the Lord) and guide you
along the best pathway for your life; I will advise
you and watch your progress.
King David
Psalm 32:8, TLB

You are good, and what you do is good.
A Psalmist
Psalm 119:68

I stood there trying to understand why my eight-year-old son was so downhearted about the brand new shirt and shorts my wife and I had recently bought. His favorite outfit was in the wash: a pair of grubby-looking, baggy shorts and a worn-out, faded blue T-shirt.

I asked him why he didn't like the new, nicer-looking shirt and shorts. He shrugged and said he didn't know, and his pouting lips showed real hurt. I tried to reason with him, explaining how nice he looked and reminding him that he had picked out the new pair of shorts himself. But I could see he was not convinced.

So I asked him for a "good reason" why he was so upset. He couldn't put one into words. I tried to help him by giving him some multiple-choice types of answers, but he only grew sadder. "I'm not used to wearing these," was his only answer. So I tried another approach.

"Steve, do you think Dad is lying to you when I tell you that you look great?" I asked him.

"No," he replied.

"I wouldn't tell you if it wasn't true," I appealed to him.

"I know," he said. "It's just that I look silly."

I tried to explain that his old clothes were what looked silly, but the new ones didn't. Then I had an idea. Having identical twins provides some unique opportunities, and this was one of them. I asked Steve if he thought Scott "looked silly." Scott was wearing the same shirt and shorts that day. (We did not always dress our twins the same, but on this occasion they had chosen the same outfits.)

"No," Steve answered.

I tried not to laugh at this obvious contradiction in his thinking. But I calmly tried to make him see that he and Scott looked the same. If he thought Scott looked okay, why would he think that he looked silly? Then he was overcome with emotion and needed to cry. It was not a cry of rebellion or manipulation to get his way; it was a cry of sorrow. So I hugged him and told him it was okay to cry. I felt relieved that I had finally gotten through to him.

Then I hoped he'd be better and more reasonable. But he wasn't. He still wanted to change pants, but would be late for school if he didn't leave right away. At this point I lost my patience. I got angry with his unreasonableness, and upset that his view of himself and his clothes was so out of perspective. I rushed him off to school to deal with his own bad attitude himself.

Later that day, I reviewed the scene. I thought of my little son going off to school sad and hurt in his spirit. As the father, with the more accurate view, I was trying to reason with my son and change his inaccurate view of himself. I wanted him to see the situation from a healthier perspective. The scene reminded me of God trying to reason with me, to get me to abandon my skewed view of myself. I saw God trying to get me to trust Him when He says, "I wouldn't tell you a lie," or "Do you believe Me?"

What frustrated me that morning was I could not seem to break through to my son. He believed what I said, but it had no significant effect on his spirit. He was so wrapped up in his little view of things that it had a hold on him instead of him having a hold on it. And I had to chuckle when I replayed his response to my question about whether his identical and identically dressed brother looked silly. But I do the same thing as a Christian. Some days I think God's other children look fine, but I don't. We are all dressed in the same righteous robes of Jesus Christ, yet somehow the others look fine but I look "silly"—because my perspective is off.

If an eight-year-old doesn't understand things the way a parent does, it is no surprise that on some days we finite, fallible believers will have difficulty seeing things the way our infinite, infallible, heavenly Father does. But when our Father tells us what is true, we need to learn to put away our human perspective and believe Him. Our Father really does know best!

YOU ARE GOOD AND WHAT YOU DO IS GOOD

I can still remember walking across my front lawn on a bright, sunny day when I was only eight years old and being seized by a fearful thought. It was the 1950s, and we lived in an ideal, middle-class neighborhood on Long Island, New York. In our neighborhood all the homes were new, parents were friendly, and children played safely up and down the street and in each other's yards. Families got dressed up and went to church on Sundays and picnicked together on Saturdays.

I remember feeling happy that day until the fearful thought seized me suddenly. The bright colors of the sky, the grass, and the nicely painted homes made me feel glad to be a kid living in the U.S.A. But that morning as I walked across the green, trimmed lawn, I thought, *What if God is evil?* I suddenly had this sense of life ending and people standing before a cruel, evil, malicious God. *What a cruel joke it would be*, I thought, *if God was not only like the Devil, but He was the Devil. There would be no hope.* I don't remember how I intellectually resolved that fearful thought as an eight-year-old. I probably forgot about it over a five-cent Milky Way candy bar and a new pack of baseball cards. But I did become more earnest about my church attendance.

We form ideas about God at an early age. Unfortunately, life's painful events often cause us to draw the wrong conclusions about God. *New York Times* columnist and Pulitzer Prize-winning author Russell Baker recounted a tragic moment from his childhood in his memoirs about growing up in the mountains of Virginia. At age five, his father died, and he was sent to a neighbor's house while his mother prepared for the funeral. He wrote in *Growing Up*,

> Poor Bessie Scott. All afternoon she listened patiently as a saint while I sat in her kitchen and cried myself out. For the first time I thought seriously about God. Between sobs I told Bessie that if God could do things like this to people, then God was hateful and I had no more use for him.
>
> Bessie told me about the peace of Heaven and the joy of being among the angels and the happiness of my father who was already there. This argument failed to quiet my rage.
>
> "God love us all just like his own children," Bessie said.
>
> "If God loves me, why did he make my father die?"
>
> Bessie said I would understand someday, but she was only partly right. That afternoon, though I couldn't have phrased it this way then, I decided that God was a lot less interested in people than anybody in Morrisonville was willing to admit. That day I decided that God was not entirely to be trusted.
>
> After that I never cried again with any real conviction, nor expected much of anyone's God except indifference. . . . At the age of five I had become a

skeptic and began to sense that any happiness that came my way might be the prelude to some grim cosmic joke.[1]

If God were not "good," there would be a cruel despair to mankind's existence. Life, indeed, would be a "grim cosmic joke." If God were a devilish and capricious deity, life would have no meaningful purpose and eternity would hold no hope. If God were not good, but capable of evil, His power would corrupt Him. A universe with a madman on the throne would be as twisted and demented as Hitler's reign of terror in Nazi Germany. Modern man, unfortunately, has often thrown out the notion of God completely — or, as in the case of Russell Baker, has bitterly turned from Him because of grossly inadequate images.

But the God who reigns is good. Our notion of Him as good is not wishful thinking. In Scripture God is "perfect" in knowledge (Job 37:16), in beauty (Psalm 50:2), in His ways (Psalm 18:30), in His works (Deuteronomy 32:4), in His faithfulness (Isaiah 25:1), and in His Law (Psalm 19:7). Because God is holy, righteous, just, majestic, good, all-powerful, compassionate, and faithful, the composite picture of God can be described by the word *perfect*. Not only is God perfect in the essence of His being but also in the quality of His actions and works. *Perfect* attests to the absolute purity of God. When we speak of God being the "perfect" Father we are referring to the goodness and holiness that govern His acts. "Perfection" qualifies all aspects of God's parenting.

Do you believe God's intentions toward you are good? Trust is severely undermined when we are unsure of the goodness of God's heart toward us. The psalmist affirms about God, "You are good, and what you do is good" (119:68). He encompasses the goodness of God's character and His ways.

The thing I remember about TV fathers in the family shows of the fifties and sixties was that they were wise and purposeful in their parenting. I think of the sense of fathering portrayed by Andy Griffith, Ozzie Nelson, Ward Cleaver, Robert Young, and then the Waltons' father and grandfather in the seventies. In many ways they were the "ideal" or the "perfect" fathers. They were a real contrast to the TV fathers of recent times. Aside from Bill Cosby's contribution to positive parenting, current TV fathers are often portrayed as befuddled, laughable characters who don't have much to offer in the way of advice or example. We need positive models, "perfect" parents who are purposeful, deliberate, and wise in their parenting to serve as reminders of our heavenly Father.

What can we expect from a perfect Parent?

PERFECT IN BALANCE

One Saturday, at a Burger King, I couldn't help overhearing the interaction between a father and his son. I had seen them come in. The boy must have been three or four years old, a cute blond-haired guy who needed all of his two little hands to hang on to his hamburger. But my heart ached as I listened to the way his dad spoke to him. Preschoolers are not the most adept at eating at home, let alone in a restaurant, and this really had his dad perturbed. The gruff-voiced dad harped at his son about every little thing to the point that the boy was so intimidated he could hardly eat. From where I sat I couldn't see the child's face, but as the tension increased, I sensed that if he wasn't already in tears, he might be soon. This father's treatment of his son was overbearing.

A short time later, as I sat on a park bench reading, a father walked to the grass nearby with two children: a girl about eight or nine and a little boy about four. They proceeded to take turns trying to hit a ball with a bat as their dad pitched. For the next ten minutes I listened, and my anger boiled. These two children spoke in a rude and unruly manner to each other and to their father! The little boy was the worst, alternating between barking orders in a hoarse voice and whining when he didn't get his way. All this time the father said virtually nothing in the way of reprimand or helpful discipline. The little boy's obnoxious tone grated on my nerves as I sat there trying to decide who I was going to get up and scold first: the brat or his pathetic father.

Both of these human fathers chose extremes in parenting. Bruce Narramore's book title *Parenting with Love and Limits* seems to say it all. In this book he identifies two problem approaches to parenting. One is authoritarian; this is the heavy-handed style of the dad I observed in Burger King. The other is permissive; this is the indifferent, nondisciplinary style of the dad observed at the park.[2] God is neither. God the perfect, purposeful Father is not subject to the fluctuating extremes of human fathers. His authority is always under control and metered with love. God grants us freedom, but in so doing He never relinquishes His sovereign control nor forfeits His disciplinary responsibility for His children.

John describes Jesus as "full of grace and truth" (John 1:14). This is an instructive contrast. *Grace* proclaims the free, unmerited love of Jesus Christ. *Truth* reveals man and his sinfulness and points to the unquestionable rightness of God in His principles, laws, and judgments. Without grace we would stand exposed in the unapproachable light of God's absolute purity. Without truth God's grace would be a grandfatherly kind of acceptance without knowledge and justice. Truth without grace would be a harsh, authoritarian rule devoid of the hope of forgiveness and compassion. Grace without truth would be boundless permissiveness devoid of moral responsibility. Our Lord is "full of grace and truth" in perfect balance. Truth allows Him to be an all-knowing, just, perfect, and wise Father. Grace allows Him to be a compassionate, understanding, and forgiving Father. He is never too harsh, too forgiving, too heavy-handed, too giving, too loving.

PERFECT IN HIS PURPOSES

One night my wife was praying with our sons. They were ten at the time, not at all interested in girls. But Judy prayed that God would be preparing a nice Christian wife for each of them. Steve moaned at the thought.

"Mom, that's a pretty long ways away," he said. So my wife smiled and said, "Yeah, I guess I should just pray that you don't have too much homework tomorrow, right?"

"Yeah, that's more like it," Steve agreed.

Sometimes it's hard to have the big picture when you're just a kid living from day to day. Maybe a lot of us are like that as adults, too. Why pray about something far off in the future when I'm worried about how much homework I might have tomorrow? However, parents are usually more concerned about the big picture than the daily grind when it comes to their children. Oh, they care about the nicks and scrapes and homework along the way, but their bigger concern is how their children will turn out in the end. God, too, is more concerned with the big picture and how we will turn out in the end.

God's ultimate purpose in the believer's life is clear from such passages as these:

> For those God foreknew he also predestined to be conformed to the likeness of his Son, that he might be the firstborn among many brothers. (Romans 8:29)

> And we, who with unveiled faces all reflect the Lord's glory, are being transformed into his likeness with ever-increasing glory, which comes from the Lord, who is the Spirit. (2 Corinthians 3:18)

God's purpose in each of our lives is to conform us into the image of Christ.

Mark Twain made this memorable observation: "When I was a boy of fourteen, my father was so ignorant I could hardly stand to have the old man around. But when I got to be twenty-one, I was astounded at how much he learned in seven years."[3] We smile at it because we remember those adolescent years when we thought we were wiser than our parents. Likewise, at times I haven't been sure that God, my

Father, knew what He was doing with my life.

I would be embarrassed to have you read certain pages in my journal—the ones where I ranted and raved at God because I didn't like the way He was directing my life. On those days I wanted to tear out the first page of the *Four Spiritual Laws* tract because I decided someone had lied when they wrote, "God loves you and has a wonderful plan for your life." "God may love me, but this is not a wonderful plan," I would growl. At certain junctures of my life, I felt that God had been a poor career counselor for me. In my momentary rage, I informed Him, "I've got a better plan."

I wouldn't mind your reading the pages I wrote in my journal after I had calmed down and was able to affirm the truth of verses like Psalm 32:8: "I will instruct you (says the Lord) and guide you along the best pathway for your life; I will advise you and watch your progress" (TLB).

I remember how God humbled me in ministry. Like most seminary graduates unleashed upon the church, though I knew I needed to grow, inside I still thought, *Why shouldn't people want to hear me speak?* God needed to work on my attitude. After a few years of humbling, I got to the place where my thought became, *Why would anyone want to hear me speak?*

Remember the story of Pinocchio—the wooden puppet who wants to become a real boy? He runs away and goes through a series of misadventures before his dream is realized. The story is somewhat reminiscent of the prodigal son, with a touch of Jonah and the whale. I'm reminded of the scene where Pinocchio finds himself turning into a donkey, with large donkey ears, a tail, and the *hee-hawing* snort to match. I think of that donkey image when I read Psalm 32:9: "Do not be like the horse or mule, which have no understanding but must be controlled by bit and bridle or they will not come to you." At times I've been like Pinocchio, wanting to become a real son but, because of my stubbornness and independence, becoming more like a donkey instead.

The Lord does not want to have to train us forcibly like animals. He wants to teach us as children.

PURPOSEFUL IN HIS DEVELOPING PROCESS

At times I wonder if God hasn't just scrapped His plan for my life. I feel put on the shelf or forgotten completely. To combat these thoughts when they come, I remind myself of the years God spent developing the great Old Testament leaders and even Jesus.

Jesus could have begun His ministry at age twelve, but God had Him wait another long, silent eighteen years or so. God had a plan to develop His Son. One verse that puzzles some, but contains an important insight on this idea, is Hebrews 5:8. Speaking of Christ, it says, "Although he was a son, he learned obedience from what he suffered." The verse does not imply that Christ didn't know how to be obedient and, therefore, had to learn. To interpret this the wrong way would be to imply that Christ may have been disobedient prior to learning how to be obedient. This is not the case. The verse means that Jesus, who was flesh and blood, went through a process of learning what it meant to live out obedience to God while here on earth as a man. Jesus did not have to learn that He was the Son of God; He already knew that. He did not learn what God wanted of Him; He already knew that. He learned the implications, the struggles, the sufferings of growing up as the Son of God in human flesh. Luke 2:52 says, "And Jesus grew in wisdom and stature, and in favor with God and men."

If Jesus went through a process of development divinely superintended by God the Father, should I not expect to also have to go through a developing process and learn obedience from what *I* suffer?

God is a responsible Parent who desires that we develop from "babies" in Christ (2 Peter 2:2) into mature men and women in Christ. He has a plan!

A GENTLE GUIDE

I could never imagine Andy Griffith, Ozzie Nelson, Robert Young, or any of those great TV fathers being cruel to their children. It would be unthinkable. But I must confess that at times I've had a bad attitude and wanted to report God for what I felt was child abuse—toward me! We need to realize that while God is a gentle Father, He is not always easy on us. Sometimes He seems harsh.

I have experienced this harshness. Once, after going through a hard, three-year stretch in full-time ministry, I came close to quitting. I didn't understand God's wisdom or His plan for me. I thought He was unduly harsh in allowing certain circumstances, and I ranted and raved at Him. *Don't You know how close I am to breaking? I wasn't prepared for this, Lord. Give me a break!* I felt that God didn't seem alarmed at how bad things had become. Some dark thoughts assaulted me during those days. After a while, I began to see God as my enemy.

Even after that situation was resolved it took three years before I was able to say that God worked good in my life through it all. Joseph's profound words in Genesis 50:20 contain an undeniable paradox: "You meant evil against me, but God meant it for good" (NASB). I cannot explain how the same set of harsh circumstances that are intended for evil by adversarial forces can be both permitted by God and, ultimately, used for His good intentions. Would Joseph have said God was harsh or gentle? The circumstances were certainly harsh. And one may be tempted to accuse God of being harsh, but He is not our enemy. At times He allows harsh circumstances in order to work out His good purposes, and at other times He may have to be harsh with us due to our own rebellion.

In Matthew 12:20 we are given a prophetic description of Christ's tenderness. It is said of Jesus, "A bruised reed he will not break, and a smoldering wick he will not snuff out." Another rendition is, "A battered reed he will not break off, and a smoldering wick he will not put out" (NASB). Bent and bruised reeds and nearly extinguished candle wicks are incidental and fragile things. A man can easily break in two a bruised reed. He does it incidentally by the natural weight of his hands parting the tall, thin reeds as he makes his way through the thicket and brush. Like grassy reeds, we may be battered, bruised, wounded people. It does not take much to break a bent, brittle reed.

We may also be like the smoldering wick. It is an image of a candle's nearly extinguished glow—sometimes fighting to stay lit against the wind, sometimes fighting for life against a gentle draft. A man can snuff out the weak flame of a candle with the pinch of two dampened fingers or an effortless exhaling of his breath. Our Lord knows how fragile we can be, how close to being extinguished our flickering flame is at times.

As God's children we often are like the bruised reed and the smoldering wick. Our Lord is attentive to our condition, and His concern is to bring us to life and to build us up. He is careful, not careless. He is gracious, not clumsy. He is sensitive, not thoughtless. He is tender, not bullish. He does not coddle us by keeping us from adversity and suffering, but He knows better than we do what we can handle and when.

When God led His people out of Egypt, He knew what they could and could not handle. God did not lead them by the road that would take them into immediate confrontation with new, formidable enemies (Exodus 13:17-18). Instead, He led them on a different route through the Red Sea and into the sparsely populated wilderness. God reasoned that His people weren't ready yet. He said, "If they face war, they might change their minds and return to Egypt" (verse 17). His people were not yet ready for certain obstacles and tests. They would eventually face war later, after God had developed them more. God in His wisdom knows the progress of His children and when they are ready to face particular tests.

The Apostle Paul wrote two New Testament letters to his dear friend and fellow-worker Timothy. Timothy was a young man who appears to have wrestled with timidity. Paul was the seasoned, veteran missionary. In one passage he encouraged Timothy to grow in his godliness and ministry "so that everyone may see your progress" (1 Timothy

4:15). This was not an indication of showing off. Timothy was not being encouraged to have the boastful attitude of "look how far I've come, guys." Instead, Paul was reminding Timothy—and us—that believers are in a process in which God wants to bring about real change so that our lives will show proof that God has matured and developed us into conformity with the image of Christ.

Sometimes we may wonder if we are making any progress. Sometimes we may wonder why God seems to take so long in the process. Sometimes we may think we are prepared to handle certain responsibilities, but God takes us on another route, a longer route, because He knows we are not as prepared as we think.

In one of George MacDonald's novels a woman meets with sudden sorrow and says bitterly, "I wish I'd never been made!" To this, a friend wisely replies, "My dear, you are not made yet. You're only being made—and this is the Maker's process."[4]

FAITHFUL IN HIS GUIDANCE

During one day of questioning God about the wisdom of His "wonderful plan" for my life, I came upon Psalm 77:19: "Your path led through the sea, your way through the mighty waters, though your footprints were not seen." God was leading His people, but they could not see actual footprints marking the way. God has a plan and a pathway for us, but because we don't see His footprints in the sand we wonder if we have wandered off course, if we have lost both the trail and our Guide.

It helps to hear the testimonies of people who have walked with God over a long time—people who can look back and affirm His purposefulness in their lives.

Over thirty years ago five missionaries were killed by the Aucas in Ecuador. The drama of that story continues to inspire people today. Olive Fleming Liefeld, whose first husband, Roger Fleming, was one of the martyred men, spoke recently about those events. She remembered struggling in prayer during the days when the search was still on: "There was always the hope that God was going to answer our prayer. But then I began to wonder, what prayer he was going to answer: the prayer for the Aucas to be reached, or for these fellows to be kept safe?"[5] She affirms today,

> As a believer I know that God has a purpose in every-thing. I guess I have learned through the years that even in hard things God can bring good out of those bad experiences. We may not see it at the time, and we may never see it. There are still a lot of unanswered questions, but I don't think I really need to know the answers. That's all part of faith.[6]

And faith comes most easily to the childlike. Two other images of God's guidance in Isaiah remind us of a father and a child. One is of a little child being carried: "In his love and mercy he redeemed them; *he lifted them up and carried them* all the days of old" (63:9, emphasis added). God has made a commitment to us as His children. And when we are old and gray we will still need to be carried. The promise of Isaiah 46:4 has become a perpetual comfort to me: "Even to your old age and gray hairs I am he, I am he who will sustain you. I have made you and *I will carry you*; I will sustain you and I will rescue you" (emphasis added).

The other image of guidance is that of God's hand: "For I am the LORD, your God, *who takes hold of your right hand* and says to you, Do not fear; I will help you" (41:13, emphasis added). We don't necessarily feel the warmth of being carried "close to his heart" (Isaiah 40:11). We don't literally feel Him take hold of our hand. And we don't see His footprints marking the exact path to follow. We walk by faith, and we feel the grasp of God's hand by faith.

Michael Quoist expressed the thoughts of God our Father in one of his *Prayers of Life*:

> You must let yourself be guided like a child.
> My little child.

Come, give me your hand, and do not fear.
If there is mud, I will carry you in my arms.
But you must be very, very little,
For the Father carries only little children.[7]

As I look back over my mere twenty years as a believer, I can see the clear hand of God in my developmental plan. Many times I've looked back and seen the wisdom of God's leading and in retrospect said, "Ah, so *that's* why You did it that way, Lord." God has a developmental plan for each of us, His children, to bring us into maturity and the quiet joy that comes with it. The most important thing is not that we know all the details but that we have complete confidence in our Father, who superintends the plan. However old we are as children of God we need that childlike trust in His wisdom. This is particularly true when our Father must do the uncomfortable but necessary parenting such as disciplining, correcting, and even rebuking us.

SEVEN

This Is Going to Hurt Me More than It Hurts You

I don't think God minds hurting us, but I am absolutely certain that he will never harm us.
J. B. Phillips
The Price of Success

God has paid us the intolerable compliment of loving us, in the deepest, most tragic, most inexorable sense. It is natural for us to wish that God had designed for us a less glorious and less arduous destiny: but then we are wishing not for more love, but for less.
C. S. Lewis
The Problem of Pain

Moreover, we have all had human fathers who disciplined us and we respected them for it. How much more should we submit to the Father of our spirits and live! Our fathers disciplined us for a little while as they thought best; but God disciplines us for our good, that we may share in his holiness.
Hebrews 12:9-10

"You just wait until your father gets home!" Oh, how I dreaded those words. I knew that my dad hit harder than my mom, and his yell was more thunderous. It was hard living all afternoon under the threat of punishment.

What do you remember about discipline as you were growing up? See if these lines sound familiar:

- ◆ "Shame on you."
- ◆ "Go to your room!"
- ◆ "Now you're in trouble."
- ◆ "Get out of my sight!"

105

♦ "After all I've done for you, this is how you treat me?!"
♦ "This is going to hurt me more than it hurts you."

I remember hearing certain lines when I was a kid. Now as a parent I catch myself saying the same things to my own kids. Though most of our parents were well-intentioned, and we can laugh about it now, there's more there than meets the ear. Our memories of parental discipline often have a direct bearing on our concept of God's discipline.

Perhaps you remember being punished out of anger and frustration—Mom or Dad just lashed out and swatted you. It seemed more like a venting of their emotions and a payment for your "sins" than a purposeful correction. At other times, you were given "the silent treatment"—a withdrawal of attention and affection. Your parents acted distant and disgruntled until you paid for your crimes. Or perhaps your parents would shame you verbally, making you feel embarrassed for failing or letting them down. Another parental favorite was exile to your room. This may have seemed more like rejection than helpful discipline.

Two things interfere with a positive view of God's discipline: (1) negative parental discipline, and (2) your "inner parent."

NEGATIVE PARENTAL DISCIPLINE

It is easy to associate discipline with negative forms of punishment. Few of us remember discipline as constructive behavior modification. So, naturally, when we hear of God's discipline our first thoughts may be of God punishing in anger, God withdrawing and giving us the silent treatment, God rejecting us by sending us away, or God scolding us into shame. To have a healthy understanding of God's discipline, we need to put aside these negative associations.[1]

When faced with unfavorable circumstances, how do you interpret them? Do you fear God is punishing you in anger? Do you fear He has abandoned you? Do you wonder how you can work yourself back into His good graces? To benefit from God's discipline we need to identify the negative associations of discipline from our past.

YOUR "INNER PARENT"

If we are honest about it, most of us talk to ourselves. We carry on an inner dialogue at times in which we encourage, upbraid, kick, laugh at, ridicule, shame, belittle, scold, coach, or lecture. While talking to ourselves is a commonplace thing, it also can reveal the impact our parents' discipline has had on the way we view both ourselves and our God.

A number of writers have identified what's been called our "inner parent." We may have left our parents' home a long time ago, but we took them with us! There is a connection between this inner parent and the way in which we were disciplined as a child. Bruce Narramore writes,

> While we are adopting some of our parents' ideals,
> we are also absorbing their disciplinary methods and
> attitudes toward our misbehavior. In later life—even
> in the absence of our parents—we automatically tend
> to repeat their methods of correction on ourselves. . . .
> This is the voice of our inner parent—our "corrective self."[2]

In many cases when we talk to ourselves we take on the role of a parent. Often the inner dialogue takes the form of our parental-self talking with the part of us that still feels and acts like a child.

What our parents told us about ourselves contributed to our image. For example, the child who was continually yelled at, belittled, and told he would amount to nothing will tend to take those comments with him as he leaves home. He may fight against those perceptions for years. They may rise up to accuse him at his weakest moments.

We can be sure that our Enemy, the Devil, will make use of all of those accusations that hurt us the deepest.

Children grow up being told all sorts of things about themselves: "You're stupid," "You're funny looking," "You're not good enough to do that," "When will you ever grow up?" Sadly, many of us have a tendency to say the same things to ourselves throughout our adulthood.

Our inner parent is controlled by our personalities as well. For instance, I am a perfectionist. Perfectionists never do a good enough job. My perfectionism can be a vicious taskmaster towering over me like a pushy, intimidating parent. This perfectionist parent within is seldom patient. When I botch something or make a mistake I can be hard on myself—even cruel. Depending on the circumstances I may belittle myself, kick myself, or scold myself. I may even call myself an unflattering name or two. On these occasions, I am much harder on myself than I would ever be with my family, friends, or total strangers.

But if I am not careful I can be the perfectionist father with my children. I have been guilty on occasion of pushing them too hard, of expecting more than I should, of impatience with their inability to do a job as well as I could. On days when I have been dissatisfied with myself, in my frustration I have transferred that dissatisfaction to my children—harping about little things that irritate me.

I caught myself in this act one night, and I became convicted about the impression I was giving my boys. As I left their room after saying good night, I commented about part of the room looking messy. Then I realized that almost every time I was in their room I made a comment about the room not looking neat enough. And while my observation was accurate, probably their room would never be neat enough to suit my perfectionism. As I thought about this, I concluded, *I don't want my kids to have the impression that "every time Dad comes into our room he leaves expressing dissatisfaction." I don't want them to get to the point where they don't want me to come into their room because they are tired of hearing my criticism.*

Then there is the other extreme—the pampering parent. This inner parent is always mothering the little child within. This parent is not demanding enough, not correcting enough. It allows the child within to reign.

What kind of parent are you to yourself? When you talk with yourself, what do you say?

This inner parent must be let go, just as our inner child must grow up. We must allow God through the Holy Spirit to replace the voice of the inner parent. We must allow our overbearing or easygoing or harsh parent to be replaced by God the Father, the only perfect Parent.

Several influences control what happens inside us: the little child (which we will discuss later), the inner parent, and the Holy Spirit. The little child within must become submissive to the Holy Spirit and the Father rather than to the taskmaster parent within.

As the years roll on in life, we may gradually realize that our inner parent dominates us. If we are not careful, our inner parental voice can take on the authority of God—and can actually be mistaken for God.

TOWARD A CONSTRUCTIVE DISCIPLINE

One day when our boys were seven, my wife posed the hypothetical question to Steve, "What do you think would happen if you never received any more discipline?" He responded immediately, "I'd probably be a bad kid." I had to laugh at his honesty. He knew just enough about himself to know that he needed some of Mom and Dad's constructive discipline.

I find that most Christians do not have a positive view of God's discipline. The older generation has a strict sense of discipline as a means of punishment and payment, while the younger generation has a few decades of two extremes: (1) permissive parenting, which has for the most part withheld discipline, and (2) the rise in the number of abusive parents and abused children. This combination has contributed to a confused and negative concept of discipline in regard to its value and proper methods. Without launching into the pros and cons of discipline and its methods, we need to affirm the clear words of Scripture: "He who spares the rod [of discipline] hates his son" (Proverbs 13:24); and "Do not withhold discipline from a child" (23:13). Scripture instructs parents to provide discipline, and God follows His own advice.

DISCIPLINE AS EDUCATION

When Louisa May Alcott became the most successful author for children with *Little Women* in the 1860s, she fulfilled one of her father's own ambitions. Bronson Alcott was a radical and unpopular pioneer in children's education. Though most parents practice child-rearing on their children out of necessity, Bronson Alcott practiced on his four daughters out of experimentation. One wonders if his severity and overbearing discipline was the reason for much of the unhappiness and self-flagellation in Louisa's journals. Louisa could never quite get away from her father. In fact, she remained single throughout her life and died within twenty-four hours of her father.

Bronson kept a detailed journal on the development of Louisa and Anna. He would set up temptations for them and then watch how they reacted. For instance, on one occasion he left an apple in their plain sight and told them not to eat it because it belonged to him. Then he spied on them to see how long they could resist the temptation. Once they succumbed, he returned and there was a great scene as he questioned their reasons for failing and they tearfully confessed.[3]

Though our heavenly Father has a detailed journal on our lives, He does not keep it out of petty experimentation. God does not set up situations in order to catch us off guard so that He can punish us.

The writer of Hebrews, quoting from Proverbs 3:11-12, reminds readers that God's discipline is proof that He treats them as sons:

> And you have forgotten the exhortation which is
> addressed to you as sons,

"My son, do not regard lightly the discipline of the
     LORD,
Nor faint when you are reproved by Him;
For those whom the LORD loves He disciplines,
And He scourges every son whom He receives."
It is for discipline that you endure; God deals with
you as with sons; for what son is there whom his father
does not discipline? But if you are without discipline, of
which all have become partakers, then you are illegitimate children and not sons. (Hebrews 12:5-8, NASB)

If we do not understand that God is a disciplining
Father, we will be out of step with many lessons He brings
into our life. If we have a negative view of God's discipline,
we will not understand God's purposes in it.

A close reading of Hebrews 12 from verses 5 to 11 gives
us a comprehensive look at the design of God's discipline.
We can summarize the truth in these affirmations:

◆ God's discipline is an encouraging aspect of sonship
  (verse 5).
◆ God's discipline is a sign of His fatherly love (verses
  6-8).
◆ God's discipline is designed for our good (verse 10).
◆ God's discipline is painful, not pleasant (verse 11).
◆ God's discipline is fruitful if submitted to (verse 11).

The primary word used in the New Testament for "discipline" (Hebrews 12:5,7; 2 Timothy 3:16) is the Greek word
paideia, which has as its root the word *pais*, the word for
"child." The verb *paideia* and the noun *paideuo* essentially
mean the training, instruction, and discipline of children.
The word our English Bibles translated as "discipline" is
a positive, constructive educational term connected with
child-rearing.

The Old Testament counterpart to "discipline" is the
Hebrew verb *yasar* and its noun *musar*. These Hebrew
words have the same frame of reference as the Greek word.

They mean "instruction" and "correction which results in education."[4]

God is an educating Father who uses a variety of types of divine discipline to train up His children.

In Deuteronomy 8 we have an explanation of God's purposeful dealings with the children of Israel. In the passage, God reveals how He led them for forty years in the desert. As He weeded out the older, unbelieving generation He trained their children, who would become the first settlers of the Promised Land.

> Remember how the LORD your God led you all the way in the desert these forty years, *to humble you* and *to test you* in order *to know* what was in your heart, whether or not you would keep his commands.
> *He humbled you*, causing you to hunger and then feeding you with manna, which neither you nor your fathers had known, *to teach you* that man does not live by bread alone but on every word that comes from the mouth of the LORD. . . .
> Know then in your heart that as a man disciplines his son, so the LORD your God *disciplines you*. (Deuteronomy 8:2-5, emphasis added)

The big picture is made up of what transpires in the routine of life. To bring His people to maturity, God was being very deliberate and purposeful along the way. He used a wilderness experience for dual purposes: (1) to punish the unbelieving generation and (2) to train a new generation to trust Him. Though the forty years in the wilderness was primarily to punish the unbelieving generation, God used it in a positive way for the next generation . . . the same circumstances, but different goals, and different results. A quick look at the meaning of the Hebrew words is helpful:

- *humble ('ana)*—to humble, to bring into submission, to afflict or oppress;
- *test (nasa)*—to put to the test, to prove, to test or

prove the quality of someone or something;
- *know (yada)* — wide range of usage related to knowing, to know by revealing or making known;
- *teach* (from the word *know*) — means simply to teach or instruct;
- *discipline (yasar)* — instruct, chasten, discipline; constructive and educational discipline.

The composite of terms gives us a picture of God as a Father who wisely designed a complete learning situation for His people. The forty years in the wilderness classroom brought feasts and famines, miracles and migraines, provision and poverty. Through it all, God's purpose remained the same: to teach His people dependence upon Him. God humbled His people through circumstances in order to test them and know what was in their hearts. He already knew, and He knew how they would fare in each circumstance. But He wanted His people to see for themselves what they were made of. Tests have a way of reinforcing behavior, solidifying convictions, and confirming character. And in the process of seeing God at work in their daily lives, God was "teaching" the Israelites His principles. In a sense, this process of the forty-year wilderness school is summed up as "discipline." Deuteronomy 8:5 enjoins the people to "know then in your heart that as a man disciplines his son, so the LORD your God disciplines you." Discipline is not simply meting out punishment for offenses. Discipline is an educational process of training and child-rearing.

It is helpful to observe the words that Scripture uses to describe the concept of God's discipline. The chart below compares the Old Testament and New Testament words in two parallel passages.

PROVERBS 3:11-12		HEBREWS 12:5-6	
NASB *English:*	NIV *English*	NASB *English:*	NIV *English*
discipline	discipline	discipline	discipline
reproof	rebuke	reproved	rebukes
reproves	disciplines	scourges	punishes

The Hebrew language employs verbal parallelism, which was a poetic device used to express shades of meanings in words. The Proverbs passage (quoted in Hebrews) uses a few different words to express discipline, words that our English Bibles translate as rebuke, reprove, scourge, and punish. You may be surprised at the word *scourges*. It literally means "to whip" and hence "to punish." This is not simply an Old Testament concept, because the writer of Hebrews is reminding New Testament believers of its relevance.

Words like *scourge* tend to give us negative concepts of God's discipline. Sometimes we do a theological shuffle to try to edit these out so that God doesn't seem too harsh. But the words are good words; the problem is that we humans associate them with negative experiences, which we want to avoid. God the Father may at times need to sternly punish His children. But He always does this out of His love, goodness, and merciful justice. This does not mean all affliction and hardship are His disciplinary correction.

I appreciate the fact that Scripture says, "No discipline seems pleasant at the time, but painful" (Hebrews 12:11). God's discipline is not necessarily "pleasant," it may be painful. But the rest of verse 11 reminds us that it can have a positive effect: "Later on, however, it produces a harvest of righteousness and peace for those who have been trained by it."

We need to consider one more passage along with these. Second Timothy 3:16 tells us about the profitability of Scripture. Though not specifically about God as a Father, this verse uses words to describe Scripture that are also descriptive of God's parenting: "All Scripture is inspired by God and profitable for teaching, for reproof, for correction, for training in righteousness" (NASB). There are those words for discipline again: reproof, correction, training. The word translated "training" in righteousness (NIV, NASB) is the Greek word translated "discipline" in the Hebrews 12 passage (*paideia*). Once again it is an educational process. God wants to use His Scripture in the educational process of our growth.

So if we look at what God does as our Parent, what Scripture does, and what God did with Israel, we find similar words and goals. The chart below shows the comparisons.

THE VALUE OF GOD'S WORD	GOD AS OUR PARENT		GOD WITH THE CHILDREN OF ISRAEL
2 Timothy 3:16	*Proverbs 3:11-12*	*Hebrews 12:5-11*	*Deuteronomy 8:2-5*
"Teaching": teaching (*didaskalia*)			Teach
"Rebuking": or correction (*elegmos*)	Rebuke; reproof (NASB)	Rebuke; scourge (NASB)	Humble
"Correcting": or putting right (*epanorthosin*)			Test
"Training": discipline (*paideia*)	Discipline	Discipline	Discipline

Once I had to discipline my sons two days in a row for the same important issue. What the issue was I have since forgotten, but I recorded my emotions that second day in my journal. I began to learn what parents mean by the old phrase, "This is going to hurt me more than it hurts you."

I remember the sick feeling in the pit of my stomach after the discipline, which was merely a quick, relatively painless spanking. It ruined my day, as I felt gloomy and upset for the following few hours. I didn't feel that way because I had overreacted to the situation, or because they didn't deserve it. I didn't feel as if I had erred in handling the discipline. But I realized more about the heart of God that day. God does not take delight in disciplining His children either. I believe that it leaves Him feeling a bit sorrowful. God the Father grieves when the sins of His children move Him to concerned discipline.

The good parent, because he empathizes with his child, realizes that he must execute discipline in love, with a goal firmly in mind. The parent who disciplines out of anger generally has lost control and is satisfying himself rather than serving the child. Because everything God does is governed by His perfection and holiness, He is a Father who never disciplines out of uncontrolled anger. But because we may have been recipients or executors of angry parental discipline, it may be hard for us to imagine that God is above such tactics. Jeremiah speaks for the fear of us all when he cries to God, "Correct me, LORD, but only with justice — not in your anger, lest you reduce me to nothing" (Jeremiah 10:24).

It is crucial that in our relationship with God we gain a healthy understanding of His Fatherly discipline, because it is such an essential part of His parenting.

How thankful we can be that God is greater than the greatest of human fathers! How thankful we can be that God's discipline is always governed by both His perfect holiness and His wise understanding of what is best for His children. Comparing God to human parents once again, Scripture declares God's greatness: "Our fathers disciplined us for a little while as they thought best; but God disciplines us *for our good*, that we may share in his holiness" (Hebrews 12:10, emphasis added). Alexander MacLaren wrote concerning the words of this verse:

> They go very deep into the meaning of life as discipline; they tell us how much better God's discipline is than that of the most loving and wise of parents, and they give that superiority as a reason for our yielding more entire and cheerful obedience to Him than we do to such.[5]

THE HARD FACTS OF DISCIPLINE

Bill Cosby's portrayal of the nearly ideal parent is one of the few bright spots in recent television parenting. Yet his own daughter, Errin (then in her twenties), was once in need of "tough love" due to drug and alcohol abuse, irresponsibility, and untrustworthiness. She admitted, "People see Bill Cosby as a super dad, but I'm proof that drug and alcohol tragedies can happen in even the most loving families."

Cosby said, "It's going to take her hitting rock bottom, where she's totally exhausted and at that point where she can't fight anymore. . . . Right now we're estranged. . . . You think you're not a good parent because you can't answer the call. But you can't let the kid use you." Then Cosby went on to express the need for tough love: "We love her and want her to get better, but we have to take a very firm, very tough stand that forces her to realize that no one can fix things for her."[6]

Even loving parents must, at times, be tough. The hard facts of discipline involve training through affliction. We do not know what the psalmist's "affliction" involved but we know he valued it from these verses:

> Before I was *afflicted* I went astray,
>   but *now I obey* your word. . . .
> It was good for me to be *afflicted*
>   so that I might *learn* your decrees. . . .
> I know, O LORD, that your laws are righteous,
>   and *in faithfulness* you have *afflicted* me.
>   (Psalm 119:67,71,75; emphasis added)

At the root of the Hebrew word for "affliction" is the word *to humble*, and the concept is of bringing someone into submission. God often uses affliction as a discipline to humble us and bring us under His submission for our good. (At this point we are not addressing what forms "affliction" may take in our lives.)

Malcolm Muggeridge, a British journalist and writer who became a believer late in life, wrote in *A Twentieth Century Testimony*:

> I can say with complete truthfulness that everything I have learned in my seventy-five years in this world, everything that has truly enhanced and enlightened my existence, has been through affliction and not through happiness, whether pursued or attained. In other words, if it were possible to eliminate affliction

from our earthly existence by means of some drug or other medical mumbo-jumbo, as Aldous Huxley envisaged in *Brave New World*, the result would not be to make life delectable, but to make it too banal and trivial to be endured.[7]

As we look at the wide variety of words used to describe the work of God in constructive discipline, we can list some helpful categories. Though there is similarity among these listed, it is helpful to see the different intent behind each.

Punitive Discipline

Basically, reaping what we sow. When we knowingly do wrong, we should expect the consequences. Jeremiah wrote, "Why should any living man complain when punished for his sins?" (Lamentations 3:39). Sometimes God must sharply rebuke us. At times this will be direct punishment, at other times He may let us reap the natural consequences or results of our sins. God is not a great escape clause that wipes away all consequences of our sins here on earth.

Corrective Discipline

Designed to correct and teach. Perhaps we are on the wrong track or developing a bad habit. God may expose an area of our life to help correct it before it gets out of hand. As the psalmist said, "It was good for me to be afflicted so that I might learn your decrees" (Psalm 119:71).

Preventive Discipline

To help us learn in areas of our life that can become problems if we are not given warnings, teachings, reminders, or admonitions. God doesn't wait until we have a full-blown problem. He uses the Holy Spirit, Scripture, and other Christians to convict, teach, and warn. God, the perfect Parent, sees our "secret sins" that we may be blind to (Psalm 139:23-24).

Training Discipline
God's training for life and growth in underdeveloped or much-needed areas of our character. The pressures and stresses of life are circumstances God uses to help us learn submission to His lordship and will. God the Father trains us in righteousness through the refining fires of everyday life. When we are "trained by" this discipline it "produces a harvest of righteousness and peace" as God stretches and molds us (Hebrews 12:11).

Too often we hold to a primarily negative view that sees discipline only as punishment for sin after the fact. Images of God as a Father who takes us out behind the woodshed to inflict a serious whipping do not foster a healthy concept of God. His discipline is positive, it is an attentiveness to the development of His child. Though there may be times for punitive measures, His discipline is always governed by justice and motivated by love and purpose.

THE RISK OF MISUNDERSTANDING

I never really understood parents saying, "This is going to hurt me more than it hurts you" until I became a parent myself. One thing we can say for certain about discipline is that young children often misunderstand their parents' motives. I believe this holds true in both the natural and spiritual realms.

On one occasion we needed to discipline our children for fighting (*one* of the numerous occasions). So I told them they couldn't watch television that night and that I would discipline them until they learned not to fight so much.

Scott misunderstood. Later, he revealed his misunderstanding to my wife. He said with obvious consternation, "Mom, I can't watch TV until I stop fighting with Steve. . . . That might take a long time. Maybe a month!" What I found humorous was that he thought it might take *only* a month to learn not to fight with his brother. I also realized that he misunderstood the discipline and to him the misunderstanding produced a real but unnecessary concern. He thought I said

"no television until you cease squabbling with each other."
But I had said "no television tonight" and implied that I
would use other measures to help them learn that constant
fighting is not acceptable behavior. I knew I couldn't completely eliminate sibling squabbles and rivalry. And I think
Scott realized that if that was my goal, it was going to be a
long, hard road.

Sometimes we react the same way to our heavenly
Father. The discipline God metes out to us may *seem* too
big and unreasonable. But we feel that way because we
have misunderstood His intent, and so we overreact and
miss what God is really saying. This misunderstanding is
our fault, not God's. Habakkuk misunderstood at first. He
couldn't understand why God was using a more sinful and
ungodly nation to punish and discipline His own people.
One wonders if Abraham, in his weaker moments, wrestled
with some misunderstanding about God's intent and heart
when he was ordered to sacrifice Isaac. What must have
gone through his mind during the trek with Isaac to Mount
Moriah? Did he at one point wonder, *Is Yahweh like all the
other gods after all, requiring child sacrifices?* God is willing
to risk being misunderstood by us in order to help us grow.
A loving parent is willing to take the same kinds of risks to
help his or her children.

When our daughter, Kim, was only twenty-one months
old, she developed a large growth on her neck right under
her jaw. The doctors diagnosed it as some kind of lymph
node problem, and surgery was scheduled. Now we faced
another concern: How do you explain an operation to a child
who is still learning English? How do you explain enough of
what is happening so that she will understand that Mom
and Dad haven't lost their senses? All the fine medical terminology means nothing to children. They look at you with
eyes that say, "How could you let them do this to me?" All
you can do is assure them, "It must be done. I know you
don't understand, but you must trust us. Mom, Dad, and
the doctors know best. It is for your good." I wished it didn't
have to happen, but that didn't matter anymore. When the

nurses took Kim from us at the cold, unfamiliar hospital, her eyes were filled with uncertainty. I knew she could not understand why Mom and Dad "made" her go through the fear and pain.

The complexity of the human body requires a surgeon with a precise touch. When the operation lasted an hour longer than expected, our anxiety soared. My thoughts turned to God, my Parent and my Great Physician. There are times of spiritual surgery when I come under the Surgeon's precise scalpel. Like my daughter, I do not always understand why. How many times have I misunderstood God's loving discipline? How many times have I wondered, *Why is God making me go through this?* How many times have I thought He was being unfair or unloving when, in fact, my own immaturity and lack of perspective limited my appreciation of what He was trying to accomplish for my good? As it turned out, Kim's operation was a success and her smile is intact. But through this process I learned what it means for a father to submit his child to something that she may not understand, even when it's for her own good.

I remember a time God taught me valuable lessons through some painful circumstances I endured at one church. At the time I could not understand why God was "punishing" me for circumstances beyond my control. I thought He was being too hard on me. He wasn't being fair. But I came to realize that even though that might have been true, God was performing surgery on me. This was an operation to produce humility, and I was the patient . . . but both the surgery and the convalescence seemed unnecessary because I didn't understand the diagnosis.

At times God seems unconcerned about our view of what is fair or just. At times He willingly risks our misunderstanding. In that church, God used circumstances to reveal my pride in some of its more subtle, ugly ways. I eventually recognized there was no easy way for God to produce humility in me, no easy way to reveal pride . . . no way except through pain—*my* pain. I did not appreciate God's surgery at the time. And I would not relish going through the circumstances again. But either Paul was a masochist, or a liar, or he knew something that I could only learn through pain when he proclaimed: "That is why, for Christ's sake, I delight in weaknesses, in insults, in hardships, in persecutions, in difficulties. For when I am weak, then I am strong" (2 Corinthians 12:10).

How wisely Scripture implores us, "My son, do not make light of the Lord's discipline, and do not lose heart when he rebukes you, because the Lord disciplines those he loves, and he punishes everyone he accepts as a son" (Hebrews 12:5-6). The writer of Hebrews tells us that these are "words of encouragement." It would be much easier for parents not to discipline their children. Good parents, however, discipline their children because they love them. Scripture once again draws upon the comparison between God and human parents: "For what son is not disciplined by his father? If you are not disciplined (and everyone undergoes discipline), then you are illegitimate children and not true sons" (Hebrews 12:7-8).

I do not discipline other people's children; I discipline my own children. They are mine. They are my concern and my responsibility. So it is with God. If you are His, He takes special care for your growth and development.

If you have trouble seeing God's discipline in a positive light, find out if it is because of negative images of parental discipline. You've probably lived at least one afternoon under the threat of those fateful words, "Wait till your father gets home!" In many cases the waiting was worse than the punishment. If you fear God's discipline as His angry punishment, rejection, or removal of love, then you will not reap the benefits of His discipline.

How do you talk to yourself? Does your inner parent have an unkindly tongue? Do you upbraid, scold, belittle, or verbally punish yourself? If you carry around a negative inner parent, you may make the mistake of beginning to think it is the voice of God.

God is a wise disciplinarian whose goal is to educate constructively. But because it does not always appear that way to us, we need to understand another aspect of our Father . . . His protection and power. God's purposes for us are directed by His parental heart. His discipline is motivated by love, and as we will explore in the next chapter, His protection in the process is governed by His wisdom.

EIGHT

My Dad's Bigger than Your Dad

◆

*Indeed, experience shows that it is only
the mature Christian man who can begin to see
a little of the "size" of his Father.*
J. B. Phillips
Your God Is Too Small

◆

*The one who is in you is greater
than the one who is in the world.*
The Apostle John
1 John 4:4

◆

*For I am the LORD, your God,
who takes hold of your right hand
and says to you, Do not fear;
I will help you.*
The Lord
Isaiah 41:13

◆

Our children had been taking care of some injured wild birds. One day, Steve's little bird became very sick. We took him out of the cage, brought him out on the lawn, and filled a tub with water to see if he would cool himself off. Then Steve sat on the lawn holding the pathetic-looking bird in a towel on his lap. I felt sure the bird was about to die.

Steve had done a great job caring for him during the past three weeks. He was willing to care for this little starling when no one else wanted to. It wasn't a pretty bird; it had a blind eye that looked rather ugly. But Steve and "Twinkle" became attached. I was proud of my son.

We all went into the house and left Steve alone with Twinkle on the lawn. Within ten minutes he walked in, and cupped in his outstretched hands was the limp, life-less Twinkle. Steve's face was as sad as I'd ever seen it as he said forlornly, "Twinkle's dead." As soon as he said the words the big sobs came and he cried quietly, but with real pain.

I wish my children did not have to feel the hurt of los-ing pets. I wish I could spare them that. But as a parent, I cannot protect my children from the natural pain of life. I can comfort and encourage them, but to shelter them from every bump and bruise would hinder them from experi-encing life as it really is. As I sat with Steve, I realized that God my Father at times just sits with me as I endure my cir-cumstances. God's protection doesn't always mean shelter from pain.

One of the biggest roles of a parent is that of pro-tector. Fathers, particularly, are responsible for protect-ing their family. When they fail to do so we get angry with them. In the original Snow White story, the wicked stepmother commands Snow White's father to take his daughter deep into the woods and kill her. The spineless father takes her to the forest but can't bring himself to kill her. The Disney version, sensing this pathetic sce-nario, replaces Snow White's unprotecting father with a nameless woodsman. In Sophocles's Greek tragedy, King Agamemnon sacrifices his loving daughter Iphigenia to the gods but later pays for it. And Shakespeare's King Lear betrays his fatherly duty by banishing his daughter Cordelia, but he too pays for it with the loss of his kingdom and his life.

We are not tolerant of Caspar Milquetoast fathers either in literature or real life. We want our fathers to be strong and protective. We want our dads to be John Waynes and Clint Eastwoods.

In her book *Like Father, Like Daughter,* Suzanne Fields recounts an incident from her childhood about her dad, who was a sports promoter: "Billy Conn was a famous prizefighter. Billy Conn, whoever he was, was not as big and as strong as my daddy. Nobody was."[1] Of course it wasn't true, but as a child it was to her. It didn't matter who this Billy Conn was, nobody was as big as her dad. I remember as a kid being in the midst of arguments about whose dad was bigger and stronger.

Scripture has the same affirmation: "Greater is he that is in you, than he that is in the world" (1 John 4:4, KJV). Roughly translated it means, "My Dad is bigger than yours." We could even go one better: "My Dad is bigger than all of yours put together."

Reconciling this truth with life's harsh realities can be tough. Many today misunderstand what is meant by God's protection. Protection does not mean isolation from hurt, elimination of pain, or exemption from trouble. God is not the great white knight rescuing damsels and waifs in distress and whisking them off to impenetrable fortresses. Christians get hurt, persecuted, and even martyred.

God *is* our protector, but the ways we experience His protection vary widely. It may seem strange, but parental protection can either help or damage a child. So God must masterfully balance the need for appropriate protection with the danger of overprotection in the life of each of His children. We must understand this divine balance (as much as we can from our human perspective) if we want to appreciate our heavenly Father's protective parenting.

I used to get nervous when my children first learned to climb trees. They usually tried before they were able to handle it well. There they would be, precariously stepping from branch to branch, perching on a limb before making sure it would hold their weight, getting stuck up too high without a way to climb down, or calling for help with a foot wedged between the V of two limbs. It would have been easier for me to walk inside and not look. But my parental instinct told me to stay close enough to rescue, yet far enough away to allow them to experience the appropriate respect necessary for tree climbing without a net.

I remember the day I reluctantly took the training wheels off our boys' bikes. I wasn't sure they were ready (or was it Dad who wasn't ready?). My wife and I took turns running behind them, holding onto the seats of the bikes as they wobbled along trying to gain their balance.

A child learning to ride a two-wheeler can be a scary sight. They scare cats, dogs, kids, other bikers, motorists, and anything in their path, but most of all, their parents. In their pride and excitement our children wanted us to let go of their seats. Inside I knew that when I let go the child would probably fall. But I realized that there would be several spills and bruised knees and elbows before my children would get their balance on those two-wheelers. So I let go and half closed my eyes to watch. . . .

This is the tension in being a protective parent. You try to responsibly protect your child and yet allow him to face the experiences necessary for growing into a mature adult. So you let him climb a tree, and you take off the training wheels, and you bear the tension of wondering if he is ready—the suspense of watching how he does even when he gets hurt. It is the same with God. He takes off the training wheels, endures the pain of watching us fall, and stays close by to pick us up—all because He loves us enough to let us grow up. (If He lets us get hurt—or even physically perish—His eternal and mysterious purposes will still prevail.)

J. B. Phillips renders James 1:2-4 like this (emphasis added):

> When all kinds of trials and temptations crowd into your lives, my brothers, don't resent them as intruders, but welcome them as friends! Realise that they come to test your faith and to produce in you the quality of endurance. But let the process go on until that endurance is fully developed, and you will find you have become *men of mature character*, men of integrity with no weak spots.

The process of becoming mature involves being exposed and tested. So how does God protect us without overprotecting us?

ASSURANCE OF PROTECTION

Read almost any psalm and you will find verses on God's protection:

> The angel of the LORD encamps around those who
> fear him,
> and he delivers them.
> (Psalm 34:7)

> He will cover you with his feathers,
> and under his wings you will find refuge;
> his faithfulness will be your shield and rampart.
> (Psalm 91:4)

> The LORD is with me; I will not be afraid.
> What can man do to me?
> The LORD is with me; he is my helper.
> I will look in triumph on my enemies.
> (Psalm 118:6-7)

Further, from Noah and the ark to Moses and the Exodus, from Daniel in the lion's den to Peter in a jailer's cell, Scripture portrays God the Father protecting His people, often in miraculous ways. The message is clear: We can be confident that the Father will accomplish His perfect will either in response to prayer or of His own free will.

But with so many miraculous examples from Scripture, we can easily get a one-sided view of God's protection and expect the miraculous to be the norm for each believer. When we make this mistake we wind up demanding a miracle or feeling confused when one doesn't arrive on time. The truth is that God is a protecting Father—not a hired bodyguard.

God's protection does not mean that we are insulated from the evils of this fallen world and the throes of spiritual warfare. Protection does not mean exemption. God's protection is personal, detailed, and meticulous, but that does not mean we walk through life behind an invisible force field through which nothing evil may penetrate. God's protection does not eliminate our vulnerability. It provides only for our ultimate security. As the Apostle Paul declares in 2 Corinthians 4:8-9, "We are hard pressed on every side, but not crushed; perplexed, but not in despair; persecuted, but not abandoned; struck down, but not destroyed."

Read the history of missions and the lives of the saints, and you will find a procession of men and women who stepped out for God, took risks, faced hardship, caught diseases, lost loved ones to disease and persecution, and often died young—their lives cut short through disease or martyrdom. In Scripture itself you will find God's children alternating between vulnerability and victory, desperation and protection. The God who miraculously freed Peter from prison during the prayer meeting in Acts 12 did not choose to stay the execution of James in Acts 12:2. Similarly, just three verses before a miraculous earthquake freed Paul and Silas from jail, we read that they were "severely flogged," thrown in jail without a trial, and chained in the stocks (Acts 16:22-26). The God who sent the earthquake to release them did not spare them the flogging.

God's protection is governed by His sovereign choices, wisdom, and plans. Yet when things go wrong and we are endangered, our fearful refrain is often the same as the disciples' cry in the midst of the storm, "Master, carest thou not that we perish?" (Mark 4:38, KJV).

As God's children we need to see His protection in a broader light than simply miraculous escape from adverse circumstances. God guards us in many other ways, and we are often unaware of how He is protecting us at the moment. We may each be surprised when we get to Heaven and God reveals all the ways in which He protected us that we never saw. Some examples of what He protects us from:

- ◆ Possible temptation (Matthew 6:13, 1 Corinthians 10:13).
- ◆ Evil and demonic activity (Mark 1:25-27, 1 John 4:4).
- ◆ The corrosion of this world (2 Peter 2:20) through

the indwelling Spirit, which makes us partakers of the divine nature (2 Peter 1:4).
♦ Disobedience to His perfect will (1 Thessalonians 5:23-24).

Elizabeth Elliot made an astute observation about protection in her book *The Savage My Kinsman.* Her husband, Jim, and four other missionaries were killed by the Aucas in Ecuador in 1956. Her statement is recorded as a part of a conversation between her and a *Life* magazine photographer covering the story at the time.

The photographer wrote in the foreword of the book:

> I wondered how Betty (Elizabeth) could reconcile Jim's death at the hands of the Aucas and the Lord's apparent failure to protect him from them. Her answer came back without hesitation: "I prayed for the protection of Jim, that is, physical protection. The answer the Lord gave transcended what I had in mind. He gave protection from disobedience and through Jim's death accomplished results the magnitude of which only Eternity can show."[2]

She had prayed for the most obvious kind of protection, the physical kind. This is the kind most of us think of when we think of God's protection. But she came to see that God gave the five missionaries protection from disobedience to God's call on their lives. He had asked them to put their lives on the line, and He protected them from being disobedient to His will.

God is our protective Father, but His protection is not simply the removal of adversity or pain. The truth is that God uses these things to make us (or those who observe our lives) strong.

ASSURANCE OF VULNERABILITY

Everyone must face that first day of school. How many moms have left the bus stop in tears after waving goodbye to their fearful little child going to school for the first time. Mom can't go in the child's place.

Most of us have had to face a neighborhood bully at one time or another. We may have told Mom and Dad about him. How many dads have wished they could go teach the bully a lesson, but didn't because they knew that sooner or later their child needed to learn to face ornery people on his own.

Just as human parents know they cannot shield their children from certain challenges, so God knows His children must face certain moments of truth. These moments of vulnerability, when we face new challenges and old fears, become steps of growth toward maturity. For the child it is climbing a tree, learning to ride a two-wheeler, going to the first day of school without Mom, or facing a bully without Dad. In all these moments the parent would like to protect the child from the potential harm, but he knows that to do so would be to shelter the child from growth. The good parent protects but does not overprotect. So, too, God protects but does not so overprotect us that we become unable to handle the real world.

Just as we turned to psalms for verses on God's protection, we can turn to psalms and see that many were written when the psalmist was in the midst of trouble.

Dealing with that pathetic boss, being shunned by ornery neighbors, being betrayed by a friend, being abused by a parent, failing an important course in school, barely getting through that first disastrous term on the mission field . . . I believe there are things that God the Father would rather we did not have to go through—things that in His power He could protect us from. But in His wisdom He knows His child must pass through this particular suffering because the eternal benefits outweigh the momentary pain and affliction. At times as children of God we will feel the loneliness of the first day of school, or the fear of being out-matched by the schoolyard bully, or the uncertainty of learning to keep our balance when the training wheels come off the bike.

Richard Wurmbrand, a Romanian pastor, spent fourteen years in Communist prisons. He was repeatedly tortured for his faith in Christ. "They broke four vertebrae in my back and many other bones. They carved me in a dozen places. They burned me and cut eighteen holes in my body."[3] Wurmbrand's story is told in *Tortured for Christ* and *In God's Underground*. For three years he was in solitary confinement. At one point, when he cried out to God to speak to him, he heard the terrible cry of another tortured victim. But to Wurmbrand God was answering his prayer, reminding him that He was with him in his pain — "in all their affliction he was afflicted" (Isaiah 63:9). There in a hellhole, Wurmbrand danced for joy.

Not all circumstances in our lives are of divine origin. We live in a fallen world, where evil men have their day and where God, at times, allows the prince of this world, Satan, to have his way. In spite of this, all of life can be instructive.

When the psalmist exclaims triumphantly, "The LORD is with me. . . . What can man do to me?" (118:6), he does not mean that we will be marked "off limits" to the slings and arrows of the Enemy and life itself. The lesson of Christ is that exposure trains: "Although he [Christ] was a son, he learned obedience from what he suffered" (Hebrews 5:8). Christ was God's Son, but He wasn't coddled and overprotected. God allowed Christ to experience life to the fullest and to suffer what all men suffer.

The mystery of God's protection amid divinely ordained moments of vulnerability is captured in Luke 22:31-32. At the Last Supper, Jesus addressed the impetuous Simon Peter with both prophetic warning and powerful assurance: "Simon, Simon, Satan has asked to sift you as wheat. But I have prayed for you, Simon, that your faith may not fail. And when you have turned back, strengthen your brothers." Peter was sifted through his denials and subsequent sorrow. Did Jesus not pray enough? Did God not answer Jesus' prayers for His disciple? For as the story goes, Peter failed; he denied Christ (22:54-62).

But God did protect Peter:

- ◆ Satan had to ask permission to sift him.
- ◆ Jesus' prayer that Peter's "faith may not fail" was answered because Peter repented. His courage may have failed in the dim light of those courtyard fires, but his faith did not ultimately fail. He believed Christ.
- ◆ Jesus knew that Peter would turn back after his moment of humiliation.

Why didn't God protect Peter from Satan's sifting if He knew Peter would fail? If He protected Peter from this sifting and failure, Peter would not have grown in his most needful area: humility. Peter was not only brash and exuberant, he was proud. It was time for the Father to allow this outspoken child to eat a little crow (before he heard the rooster crow). At times God exposes us in order to test, sift, and strengthen us. Peter needed to fail, or he would have been incapable of leading the apostles with the proper humility. This does not excuse Peter's sin, but I believe God got more mileage out of Peter's failure than He would have gained if Peter made good on his boast to stand by Christ (and ultimately Peter did stand by Christ until death).

Our heavenly Father understands the delicate balance between intervening to protect us and exposing in order to build us.

God is a Parent who never abandons us, but He gives us the freedom and exposure necessary to help refine us. We may feel alone, but we are never forsaken by our Father. Even in death, He protects our souls and holds us close forever.

The words of a famous hymn express it well:

Day by day and with each passing moment,
Strength I find to meet my trials here;
Trusting in my Father's wise bestowment,
I've no cause for worry or for fear.
He whose heart is kind beyond all measure
Gives unto each day what He deems best—

Lovingly its part of pain and pleasure,
Mingling toil with peace and rest.

Later in the same song:

The protection of His child and treasure
Is a charge that on himself he laid.[4]

NINE

The Breadwinner and the Bread of Life

◆

The spoiled child is not a happy creature even in his own home.
Dr. Benjamin Spock
U.S. News & World Report

◆

"Which of you, if his son asks for bread, will give him a stone? Or if he asks for a fish, will give him a snake? If you, then, though you are evil, know how to give good gifts to your children, how much more will your Father in heaven give good gifts to those who ask him!"
Jesus Christ
Matthew 7:9-11

◆

"Your Father knows what you need before you ask him."
Jesus Christ
Matthew 6:8

◆

The tiny bird was lying on its side, apparently dead, when I did a doubletake and nearly passed it. I was on my way into a convenience store when I came upon the colorful yellow-throated warbler on the pavement. I stooped over the bird to look for signs of life. If it was dead, I thought, it must have just fallen because there were no signs of decay or injury. I wasn't sure, so I gave it a little nudge with my foot. The bird rolled over and stood up as if it had been sleeping, but I could see from its erratic breathing and shaking that it was close to death. I watched it for a moment as it stood in one spot.

As I left to go into the store, I was immediately struck

by Jesus' words in Matthew 10:29: "Are not two sparrows sold for a penny? Yet not one of them will fall to the ground apart from the will of your Father." That little bird gave God an opportunity to minister to me that day. I had stopped at the convenience store on my way to a neighborhood park to have my quiet time. That day I went through all the Lord's promises on provision that He illustrated through birds. Once again, I was reminded of what God was teaching me and my family through the wild birds we had taken care of during recent summer vacations.

It all started with a nearly dead baby blue jay that my wife found in the road in front of our house. That summer our children took care of five different, injured wild birds. It was the first summer at the new church we were planting. The birds were an object lesson reminding us of Jesus' promise: "Look at the birds of the air; they do not sow or reap or store away in barns, and yet your heavenly Father feeds them. Are you not much more valuable than they?" (Matthew 6:26). We are more valuable than birds, because we are children of God, bought with a price; purchased by our Father through the Cross. Jesus died to redeem people, not birds. The promise is that God will provide because He values us so highly. There were times when my family and I felt as insignificant and as fragile as those five baby birds. Yet God faithfully provided.

The second summer we cared for six more birds. We began the third summer at the new church caring for five baby sparrows. It seemed providential when Judy and the kids came home with five sparrows—there are five of us in our family, so we each adopted one bird. After we settled the sparrows into their temporary new home, I retired to my study to review the verses about birds. I felt that God's signature on this object lesson for us was personal. Jesus' words took on special meaning again. "Are not five sparrows sold for two pennies? Yet not one of them is forgotten by God. Indeed, the very hairs of your head are all numbered. Don't be afraid; you are worth more than many sparrows" (Luke 12:6-7).

The sparrow is one of the most common birds. In that

sense, it is quite remarkable for Jesus to say that "not one of them is forgotten by God" and that, as Matthew records it, "not one of them will fall to the ground apart from the will" of God the Father. It was hard for me to believe that God's will was so detailed that not even a sparrow could fall to the ground without His knowing it. The promise in this passage is based upon the believer being much more valuable than a sparrow. Since God in His sovereign will accounts for something as commonplace as a bird, we can take great comfort in His personal involvement and encompassing care in our lives. If He sovereignly provides for birds, how much more will He do for those for whom Christ died?

GOD'S PROVISION AND THE AMERICAN DREAM

One of the most basic responsibilities a parent has is to provide for his child. Our Lord's promises of provision are numerous and often stated in Father-children terms:

> "Which of you, if his son asks for bread, will give him a stone? Or if he asks for a fish, will give him a snake? If you, then, though you are evil, know how to give good gifts to your children, how much more will your Father in heaven give good gifts to those who ask him!" (Matthew 7:9-11)

Jesus' words have a subtle humor. Imagine asking your father for bread and being served a stone, or asking for a fish and being given a snake! It is ludicrous. What kind of father would do that? Jesus is making a point: If even fallen, sinful men know how to provide, how much more will a perfect God know how to provide all that is necessary for the spiritual well-being of His children?

The father has traditionally been called the "breadwinner" of the family, meaning he provides for his family. Sometimes we think of provision in a one-dimensional sense: making your child happy and content through the provision of material things, entertaining vacations, nice homes, a shiny car, and if you can swing it, a college education — in short, "the American Dream." This is a fine way for parents to help their children. But parenting is much more than this one-dimensional focus.

I believe there is a boomerang effect for American Christians because we tend to "create" God in our own image. Those who see the primary role of a parent as the provider of the American Dream will tend to transfer that concept onto God. This mentality has developed in the second half of the twentieth century as American Christianity has become increasingly materialistic. When some people learn that God is their Father, they connect Him with their own human desires and assume that He will provide all that's best, brightest, and beautiful of the American Dream. Jesus' promise of "abundant life" immediately gets equated with the provisions of Western cultural prosperity. This grave mistake contributes to misconceptions about how God acts in our lives and what we should expect from Him.

Every century and era in Christian history has stumbled into its own peculiar theological pitfalls due to its secular milieu. For the baby-boomers coming of age in the last quarter of twentieth-century America, high expectations and unmatched materialistic comforts become the biggest threat to undermining sound biblical concepts of God.

God is not merely a breadwinning provider; He is the Bread of Life. His provision reaches down to nourish the inner and spiritual needs of man.

After Jesus miraculously fed the five thousand, the crowds followed Him. But He challenged their motives: "I tell you the truth, you are looking for me, not because you saw miraculous signs but because you ate the loaves and had your fill" (John 6:26). Jesus accused them of missing the significance of the miracle and following Him merely to get food. He explained, "Do not work for food that spoils, but for food that endures to eternal life, which the Son of Man will give you. . . . I am the bread of life. He who comes to me will never go hungry, and he who believes in me will never be thirsty" (John 6:27,35).

Jesus goes on to explain that we must partake of Him, for He Himself is nourishment and life. There is more to God's provision than simply the external needs of life; our God provides meaningful, abundant life, spiritual unity with the Giver of life.

SOMETIMES A PARENT HAS TO SAY "NO"

A fifteen-year-old boy had a decision to make: to stay with his mother and stepfather, with whom he had lived most of his life, or to move in with his father and stepmother. Life with Mom and Stepfather was more restrictive. They had set some boundaries and guidelines for his behavior. Life with Dad offered more freedoms. It would be more like a vacation, and besides, Dad's invitation included a gift—a new car. Faced with such a decision, freedom and the car won out.

Ask most children, and even some teenagers, to describe the perfect father and you will probably get a description that sounds like a combination of tour guide, activities director, and Santa Claus. Children would love to go to Disney World upon request, eat out daily, have ice cream for dinner, and live in a luxurious motor home so they could travel instead of attending school. In fact, that may sound pretty attractive to adults also!

God is a Father who is attentive to our needs, not simply responsive to our wants. But while it's one thing to give, it is quite another to know *how* to give. Perhaps the most important point to gain from the passage we looked at earlier, Matthew 7:9-11, is not simply that God gives "good gifts" but that God "knows how to give"—far exceeding the wisdom and generosity of even the best human fathers. This emphasizes understanding the right timing, the right need, the right occasion, and the right gift.

Most human fathers give, but they do not all know *how* to give. To begin with, while humans try to give good gifts, any number of things may be good from man's perspective. By *good* we may simply mean "good" as opposed to "evil." In this sense, there is nothing inherently evil in many things we enjoy today—cars, boats, well-furnished homes, sports, and vacations. But God's concept of good is far superior to man's. God defines "good things" (Psalm 84:11, Matthew 7:11) as they pertain to the needs, appropriateness, and effect upon the lives of each of His people. The things God gives us may transcend the merely physical; He may give us things that are spiritual and intangible.

Understandably, children view fun, recreation, and unlimited play as a great home environment. But parents need to know the value of restrictions and denials; they need to know how to say no. The dad who offered freedom and a new car to his fifteen-year-old son may think he is being generous, but he may be forfeiting his parental duty.

Our society today does not understand the value of denial or delayed gratification. On the contrary, we act as if these two *virtues* are detrimental. We conclude that being deprived is what only poor and unfortunate people must endure—involuntarily, at that.

I was in my car at a traffic light when a pickup truck pulled up alongside with the stereo cranked to the limit. The words of a hard-rock song blared out the vicious demandingness of our generation's newly entrenched philosophy: "I want it all. I want it all. And I want it now." The brash candor of the words show that we aren't even embarrassed about it anymore.

In our instant society, where so many material things are easily accessible and quickly acquired, the values of sacrifice, self-denial, and restraint are perceived as hardly necessary. A recent journal published by the American Academy of Pediatrics reported on a new illness "sweeping the nation: The spoiled-child syndrome. . . . Children exhibiting symptoms of the disease are excessively 'self-centered and immature,' as a result of parental failure to enforce 'consistent age-appropriate limits.'"[1]

Major studies are being conducted on the results of the past few decades of parental theories. These results can be seen in the lives of the subjects who are now adults. As *U.S.*

News & World Report asserted, "Spoiled children grow into spoiled adults, never learning how to delay gratification or tolerate not getting their own way."[2]

I like their term *age-appropriate limits*. It means that children must be denied certain things at certain ages in their development. Recent studies have found that neither authoritarian nor permissive parenting are the most effective. Rather, *authoritative* parenting is the best. Authoritative parents understand "age-appropriate limits." They set firm boundaries and are not overly punitive. Authoritative parents help instill in their children the understanding that many important things in life require commitment and sacrifice and the accompanying necessary denial, delay of gratification, and discipline.

In an era in which some of our Christianity has reached "sanctified" excesses and flamboyancy, we have lost the proper emphasis on God as a wise Parent who purposefully denies His children. Some, today, make God sound like an irresponsible pushover who bends to our every wish and demand and indulges our childish shortsightedness. Or instead of a heavenly Father, God sounds like a carnival master selling snake-bite oil "good for whatever ails you," and people flock to Him like spiritual hypochondriacs looking for a cheap cure-all.

Surprising as it might sound, God is not out to impress us with His miracles and power. He is out to transform us into obedient sons and daughters who will bring glory and honor to Him. Like a wise parent, God will deny us what may appear good and helpful in order to bring about the greater good. Like most children, we often fail to see the value of being denied, and we often lack appreciation of the greater good.

THE DIFFERENCE BETWEEN NEEDS AND DESIRE

How can we find the balance in understanding God's parental provision and denial? A number of verses refer to God's provision in terms of "all things." It is helpful for us to understand what "things" fall under God's provision, what conditions we are to meet, and the context of the verses we often quote. First let's list several of the more popular verses (the key phrases are highlighted).

> For the LORD God is a sun and shield;
>> the LORD bestows favor and honor;
> *no good thing does he withhold*
>> from those whose walk is blameless.
>>> (Psalm 84:11)

"Do not be like them, for your Father *knows what you need* before you ask him." (Matthew 6:8)

"So do not worry, saying, 'What shall we eat?' or 'What shall we drink?' or 'What shall we wear?' For the pagans run after *all these things*, and your heavenly Father knows that you need them.

"But seek first his kingdom and his righteousness and *all these things* will be given to you as well." (Matthew 6:31-33)

"If you, then, though you are evil, know how to give good gifts to your children, how much more will your Father in heaven give *good gifts* to those who ask him!" (Matthew 7:11)

He who did not spare his own Son, but gave him up for us all—how will he not also, along with him, graciously give us *all things*? (Romans 8:32)

God is able to make all grace abound to you, so that in *all things* at all times, having all that you need, you will abound in every good work. (2 Corinthians 9:8)

My God will meet *all your needs* according to his glorious riches in Christ Jesus. (Philippians 4:19)

Each of these passages has a distinct emphasis on God's provision, and some have conditions for man to meet. The chart below helps put these into context.

VERSE	EMPHASIS ON GOD'S PROVISION	CONDITIONS FOR MAN
Psalm 84:11	"Good things" are God's determination.	Walk blamelessly.
Matthew 6:8	God knows just what we need even before we ask.	Pray simply.
Matthew 6:31-32	God knows our basic needs (food, shelter, clothing).	Don't worry.
Matthew 6:33	God will meet our basic needs.	Follow God.
Matthew 7:11	God knows how to give good gifts.	Asking.
Romans 8:32	Provision of all the theological benefits of salvation in Christ.	Believing/ receiving Christ.
2 Corinthians 9:8	God will graciously meet all our needs.	Giving.

The simple key is to remember that God is our Parent, and He knows the difference between needs and wants. We can rest in the assurance that "your Father knows what you need before you ask him" (Matthew 6:8).

Sometimes we need to look at two opposite sides of a theological coin to get the whole picture:

◆ The head: God's provision—simply stated, God promises to provide for us.
◆ The tail: Christ's call to sacrifice and self-denial.

Both sides of this coin are important aspects of knowing and following God. Yet in some ways they may appear to conflict because I often expect God's provision to mean:

◆ I will have plenty. . . . I won't experience neediness.
◆ I won't be deprived. . . . I won't have to do without.

But this is not what provision means. The other side of the coin will help me gain some balance and perspective.

The essence of being called to follow Christ and be His disciple necessitates sacrifice.

Sacrifice implies that at times:

♦ I will do without something.
♦ I will get by on less for a higher good.
♦ I will give up something for someone else.
♦ I will experience neediness for the Kingdom and
  the King.

There is a point at which wrong expectations about God's provision will lead to wrong expectations about sacrifice. It is easy in the United States to lose touch with the biblical concept of Christian sacrifice amid all our cries of "praise God for this and that blessing." Perhaps too many have turned God's promises of "provision" into promises of "prosperity." Many promises for provision are in the context of giving and sacrifice.

For example, when Jesus sent out the Twelve He told them to take nothing, because they would be provided for. Their provision came in the context of sacrifice (Matthew 10:5-10). When Paul wrote of Jesus, he said, "For you know the grace of our Lord Jesus Christ, that though he was rich, *yet for your sakes he became poor*, so that you through his poverty might become rich" (2 Corinthians 8:9, emphasis added). Jesus made us rich, but do not take this as a promise of material prosperity. We have been made rich because we are members of God's family and partakers of His divine nature.

When Paul spoke about himself, he described himself as "poor, yet making many rich; having nothing, yet possessing everything" (2 Corinthians 6:10). And again, "So I will very gladly spend for you everything I have and expend myself as well" (2 Corinthians 12:15). For Paul, God's provision came in the context of sacrifice and giving.

Mary was privileged to be chosen by God to bear the Messiah. Yet her privilege brought with it risk, ridicule, misunderstanding, and sacrifice. Mary was specially blessed and provided for in the context of being put down, imposed upon, and inconvenienced.

THE VALUE OF BEING DENIED

When God does not come through for you the way you expect, do you jump to the wrong conclusions about Him and/or yourself? Could it be that God in His wisdom has denied you in order to bring about a greater good?

We often pray for things without receiving them. Is God not able? Is He without power? Or are we without understanding? James warns that we can pray wrongly: with the wrong motives, to please our lusts (James 4:3).

I wonder how many times parents have said to their children, "I said 'no,' and I mean 'no.'" I wonder how many times God has said it to us. God denies us for different reasons: sometimes because of our sin, sometimes because of His wisdom. Sometimes He denies us because of His own sovereign will and plan that takes into account the broad spectrum of human need and activity.

I have often denied my children their requests because I knew better. Sometimes a child's attitude is wrong or his request is inappropriate. Perhaps it is ill-advised because he does not know what he really needs. Perhaps the child is not ready to handle the responsibility that goes with the request. Perhaps granting his request will bring harm to someone else.

My children often thought they were more capable and ready to help than they actually were. So sometimes I would let them think they were helping and then, like most children, they would lose interest and leave me in peace to do the job. But I remember a few occasions, as they grew a bit older, when they insisted on helping . . . usually in the workshop or yard, and usually after I had explained to them that because of the difficulty of the chore it would be better if they didn't try. I had a good sense of what my children could and could not handle. And I often had a good reason for denying them an opportunity to help me. But because they insisted, I would give them a chance. I would stand by and watch them struggle as they realized their limitations and understood my reasons for saying no.

Moses was denied entrance into the Promised Land as a discipline. David was denied the privilege of building a temple because of God's discretion. Jeremiah was denied a "successful, thriving" ministry because of the times and God's sovereign plans. Job was denied a quick healing because God's glory would come God's way in God's time. Both Stephen and James were denied rescue and instead suffered martyrdom for reasons that only God is privileged to know. Paul was denied the healing of his "thorn in the flesh," even though he asked God on three occasions for relief (2 Corinthians 12:8), so that God's grace could prove sufficient in weakness.

Even as we ask, we must stay open to the possibility that our heavenly Father may deny our request. Persistence in prayer is one thing, but insistence in prayer amounts to demandingness. If we are not prepared to grant God His parental right of denying His children, we need to be reminded of the haunting refrain of Psalm 106:15. In speaking of the stubbornness of the children of Israel while in the wilderness, we read that God "gave them their request; but sent leanness into their soul" (KJV).

As a young high school biology teacher, my wife, Judy, often dealt with "graduating" seniors who were precariously close to not graduating due to a failing grade or two. One girl had failed all year. But like many students she didn't care that much about school and wasn't worried about a few failing grades—not until May rolled around. Then she awoke to the warning that her graduation was on the line. Her grade in one class would determine if she graduated in June with her classmates or if she had to go to summer school and postpone graduation.

The one grade that stood in her way was in my wife's biology class. The girl pleaded with Judy to give her a passing grade. But in good conscience, Judy could not "give" this student a passing grade, because the girl made no effort all year to do her work or pass her tests. Judy was a fair and understanding teacher, but something told her that it would be wrong to give this student what she had not earned. The girl did not graduate until after attending summer school.

Teachers do not always know the impact they have on lives. And often, the biggest impact is not in biology or math or English literature. But a year after this incident the same young girl, who was now in the working world, walked into my wife's classroom.

Judy was not sure what intentions this once irate student had, so she was initially startled. But the girl came up to Judy and thanked her. A year later this young lady realized the value of my wife's denial and unbending position. The ex-student explained that no one had ever really denied her anything before. She was always able to get what she wanted at home and at school without having to work for it. By denying her a passing grade, Judy provided a difficult but life-changing learning process that this young lady appreciated a year later.

"I needed that," she said. It helped prepare her for the real world. It would have been easier for both Judy and the student to grant her the grade, but the best lessons are often learned through pain.

At times God says to us, "I said 'no,' and I mean 'no.'" At other times He freely provides. We need to learn to trust and thank Him for both His purposeful denials and His gracious provision.

It strikes me again and again that in my finite condition, I seldom see the wisdom of God's plan in my life until further down the line. This reminds me that it comes back to trusting God, my sovereign Parent, and "being confident" with the eyes of faith that "he who began a good work in you will carry it on to completion" (Philippians 1:6).

TEN

A Father Who Never Lets Go

◆

*Evangelicals sometimes . . . claim God's power as the
guarantee of total change from pressure to peace, from
disappointment to joy—and then live with an intolerable burden that either crushes us with despair or
requires us to pretend we're better than we are.*
Larry Crabb
Inside Out

◆

*What if God, choosing to show his wrath and make his
power known, bore with great patience the objects of his
wrath—prepared for destruction? What if he did this to
make the riches of his glory known to the objects of his
mercy, whom he prepared in advance for glory . . . ?*
The Apostle Paul
Romans 9:22-23

◆

*But when the kindness and love of God our Savior
appeared, he saved us, not because of righteous things
we had done, but because of his mercy.*
The Apostle Paul
Titus 3:4-5

◆

I took my sons bowling for the second time when they
were eight. We went after school when the lanes were
not crowded. When we arrived, I noticed that the place
was nearly empty except for a group of handicapped bowlers
in wheelchairs.

My boys and I started bowling about eight lanes away
from them. I had never seen people bowling in wheelchairs
before, so I was quite intrigued and kept glancing over at
them for the next half-hour. They had various degrees of
proficiency at bowling and in their physical handicaps. I
could not see their scores, although I gathered they were
not very good. But one thing stood out: They were really

enjoying themselves, and it wasn't because of their scores.

Meanwhile, my sons weren't doing too well either. I coached them and tried to help them with technique. But my awareness of the handicapped bowlers, somehow, took the edge off the pressure to get a great score.

Then the handicapped bowlers left. Within a few moments, a teenage boy—probably about seventeen years old—began bowling just four lanes away. Now only two lanes were in use in the whole building, his and ours. Like many of the newer bowling alleys, here the scores were kept automatically and displayed on a large computer screen about four feet above the lanes for all to see. This is fine when you are bowling well.

I didn't take note of the teenage bowler until I heard the violent crashing of the pins on his lane. So I watched for a few moments as he bowled four strikes in a row. He bowled with precision, speed, and power. Each ball struck with a decisive, violent impact, sending pins crashing about. At another string, I counted five straight strikes. I was both impressed and intimidated.

My boys were awkwardly rolling their bowling balls, just trying to keep them on the lane and out of the gutter. They were not doing too well. And Dad wasn't doing too well, either. Years ago, as a teenager, I was a good bowler. I can usually make a fair showing, but that was not a good day. I found myself wishing I could turn off the big display screen of our scores. My boys were standing in awe of this teenage pro, and suddenly, Dad wasn't too good. The handicapped bowlers were forgotten as performance became our measuring stick.

The boys were saddened and frustrated by their failure, and I was losing patience as their coach. They wanted to do well for Dad. They wanted to show me that they could perform well. They wanted to show me that they were getting bigger and stronger. Children are so aware of growth, so conscious of size, and so ready to get bigger. And bowling looks so easy to both adults and children: Roll this big ball down the lane, hit the pins, and watch them knock into each other and fall down. But the game was losing its fun as the boys realized how far they had to go to get good.

I missed another spare and felt foolish, because I wanted to look good, too. I wrestled with myself and fought the urge to hustle myself and my discouraged sons right out of the bowling alley. But then I remembered the scene earlier when the handicapped bowlers reminded me that the issue wasn't how good a bowler I was. Before the teenage pro came in, I was simply thankful for healthy children while at the same time impressed with the courage of those who overcame handicaps. I wasn't as concerned about the score then.

As I thought about this, things began to come back into perspective for me, and suddenly, bowling wasn't that important. That exceptional bowler wasn't intimidating anymore. It didn't matter if my boys ever became good bowlers. It didn't matter what people thought of our scores on the big screen.

For me that day, the shortness of life was framed in an extended hour at the bowling alley. Our frail human condition and our years of performing to reach a certain level of proficiency are all but a short moment. In the stark emptiness of that cavernous bowling alley, there we were: the handicapped, the blossoming youth, the struggling children, and the self-conscious adult, rolling balls down a wooden floor to knock down pins and letting our scores define who we are and how we feel about ourselves. But performance is not what life is all about. It is not what Christianity is all about either. Making the grade, scoring high, measuring up, meeting the standard can become traps and false barometers of who we are. Sometimes we need to be reminded that we are much more than our bowling scores.

But sometimes I get the sense that all of who I am is displayed on a big score screen. We spend so many years growing up being rated, graded, measured, compared, and ranked that we naturally think that God deals with us primarily on a performance basis.

GROWTH VERSUS GRADES

It has been hard for me to get to the place where I can rest in God's acceptance of me. I still find myself slipping and wondering how I rate and compare. It is hard to maintain a proper balance of knowing I am loved and yet striving to please God. If I am not careful, I could cross over the line and wind up with a legalistic works theology.

Almost every avenue in life has some process of development and ranking. In school we become labeled as A, B, C, D, or F students. To go to college we have to take tests to determine our acceptability to certain schools (SATs). In college we become grade point averages. Then there are Graduate Entrance Exams (GREs), Masters and Doctoral theses, and further exams that lead to MAs, MBs, M.Divs, Ph.Ds. Many professions have licensing exams and procedures. In the military, everyone wears their rank on their sleeve or lapel—PFCs, AFCs, NCOs, etc. In the business world there are performance-based appraisals and annual salary evaluations. Much of this is fine and necessary. But the alphabet soup of ratings creates a constant air of comparison. No wonder when we approach the spiritual life we feel pressure to earn God's acceptance and even to "win" over our Christian brothers and sisters.

The pressure comes from knowing that we need to grow. We need to increase in righteousness, fruitfulness, and obedience. God calls us and challenges us to grow. Growth is the emphasis, not grades. But we make the mistake of connecting performance with acceptance. Because of that, we constantly compare and measure ourselves against each other. "We do not dare to classify or compare ourselves with some who commend themselves. When they measure themselves by themselves and compare themselves with themselves, they are not wise" (2 Corinthians 10:12).

We need to look at ourselves honestly and see our needs, weaknesses, and sins, but not lose sight of God's love and acceptance. Some people talk about God's love and wind up using it as an excuse: "Since He loves me 'just as I am' it's not that important that I change and grow." Others talk so much about the need to change and honor God that people wind up figuring they have to earn His approval and acceptance every day. One path leads to a soft Christianity, the other to a neurotic Christianity.

If we are to grow as healthy children of God, we must affirm both truths: (1) we are loved children, and (2) we are needy children who are called to grow.

DISTORTED MIRRORS VERSUS CHRIST'S MIRROR

Have you ever thought as you reflected upon your Christian life and growth, *I have a long way to go*? I have on more than one occasion murmured those words with dismay. Usually I'm thinking that I don't rate too high on the discipleship scale. Maybe you've been a Christian for a good number of years, as I have, yet you still feel you have far to go. How would you rate yourself?

It is important to note the difference between how we perceive ourselves (and others) and how our Lord perceives us. Have you ever stood in front of the funny mirrors at a circus or carnival that are contoured instead of flat? One mirror makes you look short and stout, like you've been squashed. Another mirror makes you look tall and thin, like you've been stretched. Still another makes your head look huge and your body small. Some of us have similarly distorted perceptions of ourselves before God. Instead of seeing an accurate image of who we are, we are looking in the wrong mirror.

I was reminded of distorted self-images again with our twins. One day when Scott was seven years old he complained, "I'm ugly." My wife quickly asked, "Do you think Steve is ugly?" In defense of his brother, Scott blurted out, "No!" Steve, who was in the room, reminded Scott of the obvious, "But, Scott, we look the same!" Scott hasn't complained about being ugly nor accused Steve of being ugly since. Sometimes our distorted perceptions and emotional states get the better of us in both the earthly realm and the spiritual realm.

How would we rate Christ's disciples during the last days of His life? I know I have often poked fun at the disciples for their slowness, lack of faith, and propensity for sticking their feet in their mouths. Considering their extended time in Jesus' presence, it seems that they should have done better. On a scale of one to ten, how would you rate them? During the Last Supper, they showed a dullness of understanding. They asked questions to which they should have known the answers (John 13–14). They argued after Communion about who would be the greatest (Luke 22). During the hours leading up to Christ's death and resurrection, they fell asleep when He asked them to pray, Peter resorted to violence and hacked a soldier's ear off with a sword. They all deserted Him, Peter publicly denied Him, and Thomas persisted in doubt about the Resurrection until Christ appeared to him. This hardly looks like a good track record for the future founders of the Church! From our perspective, we would not applaud them for "glorifying" God nor for being men of conviction and knowledge.

Yet in the midst of all this stands Christ's high priestly prayer in John 17. In verses 6 to 10 we read of Christ's affirming view of His disciples. Here's what He says about them: They were obedient (verse 6); they had knowledge (verse 7); they had convictions (verse 8). And to our surprise Christ says, "Glory has come to me through them" (verse 10).

I remember reading these words one day and doing a double take. *Is Jesus talking about the same disciples I've been reading about?* I wondered. I began thumbing back through the gospel, wondering if I'd missed something. Were there some other disciples I didn't know about?

Christ's "rating" of the disciples is encouraging. Jesus knew all about them, their weaknesses, and their failures—past, present, and future—yet found reason to praise them. In the same way as He looked at His bungling band of ragtag followers, He looks at us and His heart swells with affirmation. In John 17 Jesus was bragging to the Father, within earshot of at least one disciple, about His disciples.

Jesus looked at them and said so the whole world could hear, "They are *my* disciples." I may have rated them as only fives or sevens. Jesus says they are tens!

In those moments when you rate yourself low, run yourself down, and accuse and belittle yourself while the Devil cheers you on, remember that Christ is the One who eternally affirms and builds you up before the face of the Father.

But Jesus also knew how much His disciples needed to grow. God is not naive about His children. He does not whitewash sin nor ignore stunted growth. Remember, He is "full of grace and truth." In the light of His truth we are fully known, in all our sinfulness. But because of His fullness of grace, our heavenly Parent helps us grow within the context of a relationship of love and acceptance.

THE MIRROR OF THE WORD

God expects us to grow. The Bible is like a mirror that can tell us what we look like. James put it this way: "Anyone who listens to the word but does not do what it says is like a man who looks at his face in a mirror and, after looking at himself, goes away and immediately forgets what he looks like" (1:23).

Sometimes what we see in the mirror isn't flattering. But if we are going to grow we can't look in the mirror only when we have on our Sunday best. The mirror of the Word isn't designed to make us feel bad; it is designed to reveal truth, to show us how things really are.

The Bible often describes Christian growth in terms related to physical growth. Paul speaks as if he were giving birth when he speaks of his desire for believers to grow: "My dear children, for whom I am again in the pains of childbirth until Christ is formed in you" (Galatians 4:19).

The process of Christian growth is described as growth from "babes" in Christ (1 Peter 2:2) to maturity (Hebrews 6:1). John addresses believers as "dear children," "fathers," and "young men" (1 John 2:12-14). John Stott comments,

"He is indicating not their physical ages, as some have thought, but stages in their spiritual development, for God's family, like every human family, has members of different maturity."[1] The following chart lists the New Testament terminology of Christian growth stages.

STAGES OF SPIRITUAL GROWTH—TERMINOLOGY		
Term	*Reference*	*Definition*
"Newborn babies" and "infants"	1 Peter 2:2 Ephesians 4:14	Those who need the "milk" of the Word to grow.
"Children"	1 Corinthians 14:20 1 Thessalonians 2:7-8	Those still needing to grow more solid in their faith, understanding, thinking, and fruitfulness.
"Young men" (and women)	1 John 2:13-14	Those who have "overcome the evil one" by walking a consistent life of faith; they are in the battle; growing toward maturity.
"Mature" or "father" (or mother)	Ephesians 4:13 Philippians 3:15 1 Thessalonians 2:7-11 Hebrews 5:14, 6:1 1 John 2:12-14	Those who have gone beyond the basics, who are more stable, who are ready to teach and lead, those who are maturing.

When our children were two and did the things two-year-olds do that test a parent's patience, I remember expecting more from them. After all, these were my kids!

Whether it was spilling milk (which happened at least once each meal), tripping on the stairs, playing with the birthday cake icing, or having better intentions than success in potty training, our children were like most others at the age of two. But I didn't always understand this. When they were two, I caught myself expecting them to act as if they were five. Then when they were five, I remember expecting them to act seven and, sometimes, ten.

It hit me early that as a parent I can tend to set unreasonable expectations on maturity. I was ignoring the basic biological time clock. It was important for me to realize that though each child is unique in his or her own ways, all children proceed through the same general stages of growth and development. When my children didn't understand multiplication in the second grade, I learned not to panic because I knew they would get it in the third grade. There was no need for me to teach them algebra and calculus during the summer vacation. You can't really speed up time. Parental patience is essential to bearing with the growth processes of children.

I am glad that God didn't try to teach me everything about life and holiness during the first two years of my Christian life. I am glad that He didn't expect me to absorb many of the deeper points of Christian maturity during the first couple of years of my new life in Christ. I'm glad that He gave me some growing time before He exposed me to some of the harder trials of faith; I'm not sure I could have handled them too early. I'm glad that when I was only a toddler in Christ, God, in His patience, did not expect me to be as mature as a twenty-year veteran. God is a patient Father who understands the process of growth.

How patient our Lord was with His slow-to-comprehend disciples. How patient God was with Jeremiah's complaints. How patient He was during David's year of unrepentant sin. How patient He was with Peter's stubborn and prejudicial spirit toward Gentiles. How patient God was with conniving Jacob. Jacob, whose name meant "swindler," approached most of his life like a fighter. What a picture we have of God's patience as He wrestles with Jacob through the night (Genesis 32:24-30).

Don't try to spiritualize this gritty passage into some symbolic night of prayer. Both the mystery and the earthiness of God's dealings with man meet head-to-head in this passage. The Almighty God and Father, who at any moment could overpower hotheaded Jacob, instead chooses to go to the mat with His child, to roll around in the dirt and dust and wrestle out of His son's spirit the last vestiges of rebelliousness. It's almost as if God looks at Jacob and says, "Go ahead, hit Me with your best shot." God doesn't pound Jacob into submission. Instead He meets him on his terms. Jacob, who has wrestled with people all his life, fights the match of his life. God knows the real wrestling match is between Jacob and Jacob, as well as between Jacob and God. With Jacob, God not only "stoops down" but rolls around to make him great.

How patient God was with the immature faith of the timid Gideon. What a marvelous picture of a patient Father we have as God agrees to wait and "not go away" until Gideon comes back with an offering. I often wonder in passages like this what God did while He waited. Did He (in the form of the angel of the Lord) perhaps sit on a rock or lean against an oak tree while waiting for what must have been a few hours as Gideon scurried about preparing a young goat, making broth, and baking bread (Judges 6:17-22). I, too, have waited in my tracks or in my lawn chair as my children have whisked off to make mud pies or stick-figured drawings to bring back to please me.

In those moments I see God and I see myself: God, the patient Father, who with both a smile and a chuckle attentively accepts what must seem like broth and mud-pie offerings from this childlike son.

That God is patient doesn't mean that He simply puts up with us and tolerates us. He isn't a Father who waits around until we finally grow up and arrive at adulthood. His patience means that He *bears with* us, He *works with* us, and He *perseveres with* us in our growth process. He is our Emmanuel—God *with us*.

It may be easy for some to have an image of God as a Father who is not satisfied with us until we grow up. But God is not a celestial grump who does not enjoy His children.

I've noticed that some parents can't wait until their children "grow up," and they dread certain stages of the process. I remember the statement a fellow pastor made when his children were teens and mine were still preschoolers. With enthusiasm he simply said about children, "Each age has its own special joys and accomplishments." I realized that this father enjoyed watching his children go through different stages of growth, and I thought, *How much more must God enjoy His children?*

I remember trying to drill my kids in math and losing patience. "Why haven't they got it yet? How many times do I have to go over it before these basics stick? I was good in math when I was in school (until I got to calculus). Why aren't they good at it yet?" I murmured these complaints in my impatience. I was intolerant because my kids didn't catch on fast enough for me (actually they were among the better students; I just expected more). Once again I was expecting them to be two years older than they actually were.

Gradually, I began to see what was happening. In my impatience, I was intimidating them and making it harder for them to learn and respond. Dad needed to cool off and show some patience! Being patient would help the learning process. When I realized this, I felt thankful that God was a better Parent to me than I was being to my children.

How easy it would be for God to be impatient with us. People who are proficient at certain things are not always tolerant of those who aren't. Math was easy for me, so I was impatient with my children, who were struggling. It is like that in many areas. The great golfer, the pro bowler, the tennis champ, the meticulous and gifted musician are often impatient with those still learning. It may seem strange to say, but have you ever thought how hard it could be for God, who is perfect in everything, to put up with bungling, inept, sinful creatures like ourselves? God, who is and always has been perfectly holy, has never had to work at being perfect. Perfection has never been a problem for God; it's natural for Him. How easy, it would be for God to be impatient with our rate of growth.

At times God gets angry with us, but His anger is not a loss of patience, and it is not born out of frustration and a loss of temper. At times He is angry because He has a right to expect us to behave in certain ways — and we don't. At times He is angry due to His holy demands, and in His divine jealousy, He knows what is best for us. There are other times when He is disappointed because we refuse to grow and mature.

Scripture indicates that our growth can be halted at

different stages and for different reasons. Christians can in effect become perennial babes or perpetual adolescents, stunted in growth. We can also become carnal and backsliding. The writer of Hebrews describes his listeners as "slow to learn" and warns:

> In fact, though by this time you ought to be teachers, you need someone to teach you the elementary truths of God's word all over again. You need milk, not solid food! Anyone who lives on milk, being still an infant, is not acquainted with the teaching about righteousness. But solid food is for the mature, who by constant use have trained themselves to distinguish good from evil. (Hebrews 5:12-14)

The writer implies that the Scriptures contain both milk and solid food, which can provide a diet for "infants" as well as mature believers. A believer's growth is also affected by growth in righteousness and discernment.

Throughout the New Testament the believer is cautioned about growth being arrested. The following chart highlights passages that indicate stages we can get stuck in.

GROWTH STOPS ALONG THE PATH TO MATURITY		
Arrested Growth	*Reference*	*Related to*
Perennial babies	1 Peter 2:2	*No foundation*; never growing in the Word of God (may be compared to one who has no root — Matthew 13:20-21).
	Ephesians 4:14	*No understanding*; always susceptible to "every wind of doctrine."
Immature infants	1 Corinthians 3:1	*No maturity in godliness*; called "carnal," infants, worldly, unspiritual.
Perpetual adolescents	Hebrews 5:11-14	*Not ready to teach*; slow to learn, should be adults but still not able to move beyond "elementary" teachings.
Mid-life crisis in faith	2 Timothy 4:10	*Compromised convictions*; have decided not to follow Christ any longer to one extent or another.

We need to take an honest look in the mirror of God's Word and see how we need to grow. God loves us, and He is committed to our growth (Philippians 1:6). If we are "children" in Christ, we need to grow through studying Scripture and learning to know God. The Word of God is fundamental to growth throughout our Christian life. If we have been growing, we need to continue on toward the goal of becoming teachers and fathers and mothers in the faith. We need to grow in righteousness. If we have walked with God for some time, perhaps we need to "go on to maturity" (Hebrews 6:1) and grow in our service and in the continued refinement of our character. For Paul the goal was clear: to "present every man complete in Christ" (Colossians 1:28, NASB).

I remember wondering about God's commitment to me one day. I wound up reading Isaiah 46:4 in my devotions. God says to His people: "Even to your old age and gray hairs I am he, I am he who will sustain you. I have made you and I will carry you; I will sustain you and I will rescue you." What a great promise! You may not have gray hair yet, but when you hit old age, whether or not you have any hair left to turn gray, God will still be committed to you.

I like *The Living Bible* paraphrase: "I will be your God through all your lifetime, yes, even when your hair is white with age. I made you and I will care for you. I will carry you along and be your Savior." God carries us along as little children and, even after years of growing into "the whole measure of the fullness of Christ" (Ephesians 4:13), He is still carrying us when our hair is white with age.

PART III

Learning to See How God Is Parenting You

ELEVEN

Growing Pains

◆

Wendy, I ran away the day I was born. . . . It was
because I heard Father and Mother . . . talking
about what I was to be when I became a man. . .
I don't want ever to be a man. I want always to be
a little boy and to have fun.
Peter Pan

◆

Brothers, stop thinking like children. In regard to evil
be infants, but in your thinking be adults.
The Apostle Paul
1 Corinthians 14:20

◆

Be diligent . . . so that everyone
may see your progress.
The Apostle Paul
1 Timothy 4:15

◆

I took my sons bowling again. On this occasion, Scott did great and Steve did poorly. Yet they are identical twins, similar in many ways. I sat there as the father-coach wondering why Scott seemed stronger and more coordinated while Steve seemed unable to handle the ball. Same size, same strength, same experience factor—but one caught on quickly, the other struggled. Yet just the day before in a high-jump game, Steve flew over the bar and Scott looked clumsy.

I was getting frustrated with my son's awkwardness at bowling. I kept trying to coach him, but nothing worked. The ball went in the gutter eight out of ten times. When it did hit the pins, only a few fell.

He was getting upset, and I was already upset. I wanted

him to do well, and he wanted to do well. His frustration was accented by watching his brother do so much better and making it look easy. I finally gave up coaching him. Unfortunately, I let my frustration show, and it appeared like disappointment.

I was convicted of my own poor parenting and my lack of patience. *Give him time*, I thought. *Don't be in such a hurry. Let him work it out. Be supportive. Don't compare him to his brother. It's only a game.* But I had already blown it that day. I had said the wrong things; or at least, they came out the wrong way. I had shown the wrong attitude.

But then I managed to see something God was trying to teach me. I realized that I tend to see God reacting to me the way I reacted to my son. I tend to see God as the frustrated coach throwing up His hands in dismay with me, the underachiever.

I thought of a pastor I had been comparing myself with. I saw myself as the struggler in comparison to him. I was the poor bowler, he was the natural. He was good and confident, and things seemed to come easily for him. I was uncoordinated and clumsy, and as with my son that day, things seemed to go from bad to worse. And I was afraid that God would do with me just what I had done with my son that afternoon . . . get a bit disgusted, lose patience, and give up on me. I am thankful that God is a more perfect Parent than I could ever hope to be.

As the father of twins, I love each of my sons with the same intensity. I have never loved one more than the other. And I've worked hard to make sure the boys don't feel less special because of their cute, little sister, Kim. Watching identical twins grow has given me a good lesson in how people can look the same but still have their differences. I have become sensitive to the increased potential for damaging comparisons. I have been sensitive to the need to treat them each the same, but as individuals. This has helped me see that God's love for us is the same, but He works with us each as individuals.

As we grow we experience growing pains. It would be

great if we could all do well the first time we tried something—like bowling, or water skiing, or foreign languages, or teaching a class, or preaching a sermon. But we will go through times when we are spiritually awkward and clumsy. Times when we wonder why others are doing well, but we seem to be having difficulty with everything. God understands the simple fact that all children grow at different rates with different strengths and weaknesses.

We start as "newborn babies" in Christ (1 Peter 2:2) and go through various stages of spiritual childhood and adolescence and reach different levels of maturity. But the length of the process is not meant to grieve us over our inability to realize the ideal. Sometimes the process is slow and painful, but the results are guaranteed: "Being confident of this, that he who began a good work in you will carry it on to completion" (Philippians 1:6). We don't have to grow up on our own.

THE GROWING PAINS OF RESPONSIBILITY

Remember the Peter Pan story? Peter Pan was the adventurous boy who never grew old. He symbolizes the essence of childhood and awakens the child in us all. But the original play and story by James M. Barrie had a darker side to it, also. The tragic side of Peter Pan was that he didn't want to grow up. There is a good side to childhood that we can take with us as adults, but it is tragic to see adults who have never grown up and put away "childish things."

The phenomenon is so prevalent today among American men that Dr. Dan Kiley has addressed it in a book entitled *The Peter Pan Syndrome*.[1] The Peter Pan syndrome occurs in the spiritual realm as well. Christians can remain spiritual children who never quite grow up—because it hurts to grow up, in many ways it would be easier to stay a child. My wife and I have witnessed it with our children. They want to stay kids, but they can't.

A large part of the failure to grow up in both the physical and spiritual world is a lack of responsibility. We noticed this, also, with our children. The longer we waited to teach certain responsibilities, the harder it was for them and for us. Children don't often understand the consequences of not being responsible. Most parents wish they had a nickel for every time they reminded their children to pick up something. Making their bed, cleaning their room, picking up their clothes, taking out the garbage, brushing their teeth, and taking a shower . . . these are all little things, but little things weave together to form the tapestry of our lives.

Scripture addresses responsibility in various ways: accountability, stewardship, faithfulness, duty. Many of Jesus' parables are about how people responded when entrusted with a responsibility or possession. God expects us to take responsibility for our actions, sins, attitudes, thought life, other people, service, and knowledge of Scripture and God. Scripture makes it clear more than once that "each of us will give an account of himself to God" (Romans 14:12; see also Matthew 12:36, 18:23; Luke 12:48; 1 Peter 4:5). We believers will not be judged in light of our salvation, but for "the quality of each man's work" (1 Corinthians 3:13). Notice it doesn't say the quantity. It will not be a contest to see who has the biggest and shiniest work. God will be judging what we did with what He gave us. Did we give our life to eternal things that count or to "wood, hay, or straw" (1 Corinthians 3:12-15)?

Yet taking responsibility involves pain, risk, and vulnerability. Responsibility for me as a believer involves moving beyond the confines of my own, little, self-centered world into the world of others. When Jesus ascended He gave the Great Commission to "go and make disciples of all nations" (Matthew 28:19, Mark 16:15). It is my responsibility as a believer, entrusted to me by my Lord. The more I move spiritually beyond the infancy stages into an adult Christianity, the more I will assume responsibility for others and myself. And the more responsibility I realize as a believer, the more it will cost me personally. But the more it costs me on behalf of Christ, the greater the rewards I will reap in the richness of my relationship with God.

THE GROWING PAINS OF EXPECTATIONS

As a father, I want my children to do things well. I want them to try hard and be successful as they grow. I want them to do their best and be the best they can be. I have expectations for them, not so much in the way of careers and jobs but in the way of character, behavior, and values.

God has expectations of us. Our Father also wants His children to do their best. He wants us to "press toward the mark," "fight the good fight," "be ye holy," "come out from their midst," and "seek first the kingdom of God." God expects many of the same things from us that a human father would expect from his children.

There is a difference between "childish" and "childlike." Being "childish" is negative; it refers to immaturity and things not appropriate to adulthood. But "childlike" is positive; the believer is encouraged to have valuable childlike qualities.

WHAT DOES GOD EXPECT OF HIS CHILDREN?		
1. *To Honor*	"If I am a father, where is the honor due me?"	
	Psalm 45:11	Malachi 1:6
	Proverbs 3:9	John 5:23
2. *To Obey*	"If anyone loves me, he will obey my teaching."	
	1 Samuel 15:22	Jeremiah 7:23, 11:4
	Psalm 119:34,67	John 14:23, 15:10
3. *To Love*	"Love the LORD your God with all your heart."	
	Deuteronomy 6:5	John 14:23-24, 15:9-11
	Psalm 31:23	
4. *To Please*	"Live in order to please God."	
	Romans 12:1	2 Timothy 2:4
	2 Corinthians 5:9	Hebrews 11:6, 13:21
	1 Thessalonians 4:1	
5. *To Imitate*	"Be imitators of God."	
	Matthew 5:48	1 Thessalonians 1:6
	Ephesians 5:1	

As a father, I have been amazed by how much my children want to please me. My wife and I didn't teach them that. I remember times when the three of them were in a room with me and I would ask for something from my room. It became a race to see which one could get it and bring it to Dad. The two who didn't have it would wind up down in the mouth; the winner would be pleased to be able to help Dad. After this happened a few times, I learned to ask each of them to do something so they could all feel honored to do something to please Dad.

When Judy would buy a gift for each of them to give Dad for a holiday, it wasn't good enough for Scott. He would go to his room and make something or choose one of his own toys or artwork and wrap it himself in newspaper, so he could give me something that showed his own effort and love.

I have always felt honored by my children. Whenever I come home I am greeted by three who often run to me as I come through the door. Dad coming home is an event. My wife, Judy, has told me that they "adore" me. I smile sheepishly, but inside my heart swells to know that.

My children are quick to imitate Judy and me (sometimes in the wrong ways). If we do something, they want their turn to try. And they are often puzzled if they can't immediately do it as well as Mom and Dad.

Most children want to please their parents. Most children naturally love their parents. Seeing these qualities in my children helps me understand why Jesus said that we needed to be like little children. We need to nurture that childlike admiration toward our heavenly Father.

All of God's expectations of us begin with the heart's attitude. When we come to God like children with hearts that want to please, then obeying and imitating God will find their proper expression.

Reaching these goals is a lifelong process. We are called to them daily. God has high expectations of us because to have anything less would not befit His character. But there are inevitable pains and disappointments in any relationship where there are high expectations. God knows it's a process. He also knows, as James says, "We all stumble in many ways" (3:2). He knows our growing pains are inevitable.

THE GROWING PAINS OF EXERCISE

Occasionally at night our children would complain of pains in their legs or chest. At one point, I remember becoming really concerned and imagining the worst. So I asked Judy to call our doctor. He dismissed it all as "growing pains." There are times when a child's body grows so fast that they have pains in their legs, arms, chest, bones, and muscles.

I remember the pain of leaving my first pastoral position. I felt all the anger and sadness of failure, betrayal, and rejection. I felt I had failed my family, my friends, and most of all, my God. Though I knew in my heart that God could use painful trials, at the time, I did not see how He could use this pain.

In my search for another pastoral position, I told God that I wanted to go someplace where there weren't many problems and conflicts. I wanted to be where I could just "do the ministry" and grow. God was faithful to open doors and lead us to a wonderful, growing church. When I first stepped into this next pastoral position, I felt God had answered my prayer.

Sometimes we are all ready to "do the ministry" and "serve God," but God has another agenda. We think our plans for God and the ministry are the most important thing, but God, at times, makes the ministry wait because of what He needs to do with the man first. God's agenda is refinement and growth. "Character before career." It wasn't long before I realized that this new church had its problems, also. (It takes some of us a while to let go of our idealism about "perfect" churches.) I found myself in the middle of conflict again. At first, I couldn't understand why God hadn't placed me where I could just "do the ministry" instead of fighting fires, debating job descriptions, and shuffling roles and ministry hats. But God's placement service has its special wisdom.

I remember praying about my confusion one afternoon in a park. God was exposing my weaknesses and deficiencies once more, and it was painful. The pressure was still on even though I had changed churches. I realized that day that God in His graciousness was letting me go through growing pains. God kept the heat on to continue the cooking, and I was feeling roasted. Sometimes God allows pressure to continue in our lives so that He can expose our weaknesses and stretch us so we grow.

The parallels between physical growth and spiritual growth have been instructive for me. As I sat that day in the park, I thought of what it is like when someone who is out of shape goes to a trainer to get into a personalized fitness program. The trainer points out the weak parts of the person's body that need work. In the same way, if we want to get in shape, we must take an honest look in the mirror. Our heavenly Instructor will design exercises to isolate the development of particular muscles. We develop strength by exercising these muscles to the point of pain and fatigue. That's the key. To build muscle, body builders must exercise through the pain to the point of near exhaustion. You see, there is good pain and bad pain. When a muscle is strained and hurt, we experience bad pain and must stop exercising. But good pain is the burning sensation we feel when a muscle is working hard. If we stop whenever we have good pain, we will never build strength. But whether the pain is good or bad, it is pain and it hurts.

There in the park, I realized that God had isolated some problem areas that needed work. He was keeping me in the gym overtime. Exposing weak areas is an integral part of the growth process. The pressurized circumstances of life become the means God uses to exercise us through the good pain, developing strength. God is tenacious about our growth. He is more committed to it than we are. And He is often more patient than we are with how long it takes.

We have made a mistake today by not giving proper respect to the time factor in the Christian's growth and development process. Some seem to think that if we have a heart to serve God, that's all we need in order for God to use us. There is truth in that, but it doesn't say enough about the process.

After seminary I had planned to do a year-long internship at a church. I remember explaining that to a fellow student who dismissed the idea as a waste of time. He said, "I just want to get out and do the ministry. I'm ready. I don't need an internship." I felt sad for him. Perhaps he was more "ready" than I was, but I doubt it. What really counts as readiness for God comes through the pain of realizing we could never be ready enough for God. When Moses thought he was ready, God said he wasn't. After forty years of herding sheep in the desert, Moses said he wasn't ready anymore. That's when God said, "Now you're ready."

When I think back to my earlier years and stages as a Christian, I am embarrassed about some of the things I said and did "for God." Though I was sincere and God used me in spite of myself, I realize that my lack of growth limited what God could do through me.

It hurts to grow. Growing in responsibility can be a painful process. Meeting a Father's high expectations can be difficult even when done out of a heart of love. And stretching and exercising spiritual muscles brings pain . . . but it can be good pain.

I like the way Oswald Chambers put it: "Why does God take such a long time? Because of what He is after . . . 'bringing many sons to glory.' It takes a long time to make a son."[2]

TWELVE

The Weaning Process (Part 1)

◆

To the weaned child his mother is his comfort
though she has denied him comfort.
Charles H. Spurgeon
The Treasury of David

◆

But I have stilled and quieted my soul;
like a weaned child with its mother.
King David
Psalm 131:2

◆

To an infant, being weaned must seem an odd and even a cruel time. Suddenly your mother denies you the comfort of nursing and the sustenance of her milk, which you've grown accustomed to. You cry, not understanding why this has to happen. Yet you survive and grow closer to your parent in more mature ways. This weaning process in physical life parallels a similar weaning process in the believer's spiritual growth.

Weaning may be a difficult process for believers because many of us have a hard time understanding the concepts of self-denial and God's parental role in denying His children.

Christianity has courted a fascination with a Madison Avenue-style gospel that offers power, fulfillment, and prosperity. It sounds exciting, and no one in all honesty could possibly be against this alluring trio of promises. At least not at first. But there is something disturbing about it all. It sounds too easy. There is none of Jesus' talk about "denying" yourself and nothing of the "hard sayings" that caused people to stop following Jesus as they did in John 6. That kind of talk doesn't market well today. We are told to be "positive" and "possibility" thinkers. Jesus would never make it on Madison Avenue.

In this process of God's parenting we have a responsibility, and God does, too. For our part, there is no discipleship and no following Christ on to maturity without self-denial. Self-denial puts a large responsibility upon each of us—a responsibility that we are not often able to handle. Self-denial is not easy for those of us in today's world who are used to an unconscious self-indulgence and who rarely have to come to grips with delaying gratifications. At times we don't know what to deny ourselves. Often, we don't know how. So God denys us certain things to help our growth process when our own self-denial wavers. This may sound unpopular in a time when people preach "prosperity" and "power." But I believe this weaning process is an essential part of our growth. God's objective in this is to: (a) deepen our relationship with Him, (b) purify our trust, and (c) teach us contentment.

UNDERSTANDING "WEANING"

To be weaned is to learn to detach or alienate oneself and one's affections from an object of desire. Being weaned may not be enjoyable. But it is necessary, for without it a child would never grow to maturity. Our heavenly Father wants His children to be mature, not nursing babies.

Artur Weiser in his commentary on psalms explains that the Christian is . . .

> not like an infant crying loudly for his mother's breast, but like a weaned child that quietly rests by his mother's side, happy in being with her. . . . And just as

the child gradually breaks off the habit of regarding
his mother only as a means of satisfying his own
desires and learns to love her for her own sake, so the
worshipper after a struggle has reached an attitude
of mind in which he desires God for himself and not
as a means of fulfillment of his own wishes. His life's
centre of gravity has shifted. He now rests no longer in
himself but in God.[1]

David first gave a spiritual connotation to weaning in
Psalm 131:2. He says his soul is "like a weaned child with
its mother." This describes a believer's restful relationship
with God. As Eugene Peterson put it: "Christian faith is not
neurotic dependence but childlike trust. We do not have
a God who forever indulges our whims but a God whom
we trust with our destinies."[2] The process of weaning, of
growing from infantile faith to a more mature relationship
with God, has been noted by other writers as well. Charles
Spurgeon wrote,

> To the weaned child his mother is his comfort though
> she has denied him comfort. It is a blessed mark of
> growth out of spiritual infancy when we can forego
> the joys which once appeared to be essential, and can
> find our solace in him who denies them to us: then
> we behave manfully and every childish complaint is
> hushed.[3]

During my early years as a believer, God was working
in a unique way in my life. Then I reached a point where it
seemed harder. It wasn't that the joy was gone, nor had my
desire evaporated. But it seemed that God was not answering
the same little prayers the same way nor was He providing
the same sense of elation. I wondered what was wrong. I've
since discovered that this is not an unusual phenomenon.
I began to learn that there comes a time when God calls
us to a deeper maturity, a time when He weans us. Eugene
Peterson acknowledged this transition in the believer's life:

The early stages of Christian belief are not infre-
quently marked with miraculous signs and exhil-
arations of spirit. But as discipleship continues the
sensible comforts gradually disappear. For God does
not want us neurotically dependent upon him but
willingly trustful in him. And so he weans us.[4]

Oswald Chambers writes about how God may bring us
through a time when we feel separated from His comfort. In
this way, He helps us learn to walk by faith not by sight.

Inner desolations serve a vital purpose in the soul of
a Christian. It is expedient that the joys of contact
be removed that our idea of the Christian character
may not be misplaced. In the early days of spiritual
experience we walk more by sight and feelings than by
faith.[5]

AREAS OF WEANING

What does God wean us from? Depending on our individual
needs, God may have to wean us from any number of things
that we depend on instead of Him. In these next two chapters we will look at eight areas of weaning.

Our Personal Aspirations

We know from history that King David was a man of great
accomplishment and ambition. But he wrote Psalm 131 with
the relaxed sigh of a man who knows the peace of surrender
through weaning.

My heart is not proud, O LORD,
    my eyes are not haughty;
I do not concern myself with great matters
    or things too wonderful for me.
But I have stilled and quieted my soul;
    like a weaned child with its mother,
    like a weaned child is my soul within me.
        (verses 1-2)

A weaned child is content just to be *with* his mother. Prior to weaning, the child saw the mother less as a person and more as a need-meeter responsive to his demands. David's image gives us a vivid sense of a man who is content with God. Gone is the compulsive and obsessive need to feed off life, self, other people, and God.

God often uses people at specific times to do great things for the Kingdom. At other times, He calls them to be plodders—to keep walking against the current of their time, seemingly making little headway if measured on a grand scale. It was to be like this for Baruch, Jeremiah's scribe. Due to the historical circumstances and God's immediate plans, God cautioned Baruch: "Should you then seek great things for yourself? Seek them not" (Jeremiah 45:5). This verse is not to be taken out of context and applied to all of us as a warning against having personal aspirations, for without them we would never accomplish anything. But it is an example of how, at times, we must give up our personal ambitions for God.

This was a hard lesson for me to learn, especially in an age in which "bigger is better" and success is the measure of a man's worth. It is hard when God sets about to purify your ambitions. Like many pastors, I came out of seminary with great dreams. I wanted to do great things for God. But God had His own plans. He let me stumble and fall flat on my face more than once. The questions flooded in: What went wrong? Who's to blame? Why did God allow this? Has He rejected me? Will He put me on the shelf? What can I learn from this?

Sometimes our failures are not totally our fault. We may find any number of excuses or reasonable explanations. But sometimes God isn't interested in all that; He may simply be weaning us. A. W. Tozer's words are convicting: "God may allow His servant to succeed when He has disciplined him to a point where he does not need to succeed to be happy. The man who is elated by success and cast down by failure is still a carnal man."[6]

Some people are workaholics—driven, energetic go-getters by nature. They are achievers and producers. When they become Christians they apply that same energy to Christian things. It is a good quality, but it has a dangerous side. In our flurry of achievement we need to ask ourselves: Is this sanctified ambition, or is it my own need for accomplishment and achievement? Many people work hard "for the Lord," but underneath it all, it is more their own pursuit and pride.

To clothe our human need for ego-fulfilling accomplishments with Christian trappings is an understandable, yet subtle, temptation. Only after we have been weaned of our own personal aspirations can God clearly trust us to dream His dreams.

Many famous missionaries served long and hard before they saw real fruit from their ministries. We don't always know why God does what He does, but their faithful examples remind me that God is more concerned with our character than with "successful" results for the Kingdom.

William Carey has been called "the Father of Modern Missions." But he had a slow start. In fact, after his first seven years of mission work in Bengal, India, he left for another location in 1800 without being able to claim one convert. Adoniram Judson, considered America's first missionary, landed in Rangoon, India, in 1813. After six difficult, frustrating years, he finally won his first convert. Robert Morrison, the first Protestant missionary to China, took seven years to win his first convert. Hudson Taylor, founder of the China Inland Mission, arrived in Shanghai, China, in 1854. At the end of his first six years, after many setbacks, hardships, and little success to show for it all, he went home to England due to illness with many of his hopes and expectations dashed. Yet he returned with a renewed vision and went on to become an extraordinary missionary and believer. These are just a few of many examples.

In his painfully honest autobiography *The Price of Success*, J. B. Phillips details how God dealt with him. Fueled by his drive to succeed, Phillips preached and wrote commentaries, books, and even a Bible translation. But later in life, it all came to a halt as his creative springs dried up, depression set in, and a pervasive sense of the loss of God clouded his thoughts. The opening page of his book sums it up:

> I was not nearly so aware of the dangers of success. The subtle corrosion of character, the unconscious changing of values and the secret monstrous growth of a vastly inflated idea of myself seeped slowly into me. Vaguely I was aware of this and, like some frightful parody of St. Augustine, I prayed, "Lord, make me humble—but not yet."
>
> I can still savour the sweet and gorgeous taste of it all—the warm admiration, the sense of power, of overwhelming ability, of boundless energy and never failing enthusiasm. I still do not regret it; in a sense it was inevitable, for I was still very young for my age. But it is very plain to me now why my one man kingdom of power and glory had to stop.[7]

God may let us fail, deny us success, and even frustrate our "spiritual" plans in His parental concern that we purify our motives and aspirations.

Our Circumstantial Blessings

I've pictured John the Baptist's perplexed and vacant stare as he slouched back down in his jail cell. His disciples had just relayed to him Jesus' response to his inquiry: "Are you the Messiah?" In those first moments, Jesus' words may have sounded like both a yes and a no.

John knew the images from Isaiah about the Messiah's ministry. And Jesus knew that John knew them. They were images of the blind receiving sight, the lame walking, the deaf hearing, and of particular interest to John: prisoners being released. John's question probably belied another, more urgent question, which may have been, "If you are the Messiah, why am I still in this jail cell?"

Jesus' reply to John is remarkable for what it leaves

out. Jesus mentions several of Isaiah's promises that He has fulfilled (Matthew 11:4-6), but He specifically leaves out any reference to prisoners being released. As John sat alone with this answer, he realized, *Yes, this is the Messiah, but no, I will not be freed from this prison as I had hoped.* No wonder John faced misgivings about Christ and wrestled with doubts. Shortly after this, he was beheaded. In spite of John's brief moment of doubt, Jesus declares, "Among those born of women there is no one greater than John" (Luke 7:28).

When God weans us off circumstantial blessings, He brings us to a solitary place where we come to grips with where our real peace and security lie. When an unfavorable turn of circumstances dashes our hopes, we come to realize that there is often a great distance between trusting in *who* God is and trusting in *what* He does for us. He may not do exactly what we want, but He is still and always will be the Messiah.

There are times in all of our lives when the very thing we hope God will do does not come true for us, times when the blessing we think we need most seems to elude us. As believers we can get so excited about God's circumstantial blessings that we get a bit ruffled when things don't quite go smoothly. When God weans us from our dependence upon circumstantial blessings, He purifies our motives for following Him. We must ask ourselves, am I following Him because of what He does for me or because of who He is? I like the way Larry Crabb put it: "Enjoying the sought after blessings of God is sometimes confused with enjoying His Person."[8] At times, for our own good, we need to be weaned off our dependence upon circumstantial blessings. This weaning helps anchor our hopes and expectations solely in God.

Our "Hedge of Protection"

In perhaps one of the most perplexing lines in Scripture, God asked Satan, "Have you considered my servant, Job?" If we didn't know better, we would suspect that Satan provoked God and set up Job when he cunningly challenged,

"Have you not put a hedge around him and his household and everything he has? . . . But stretch out your hand and strike everything he has, and he will surely curse you to your face" (Job 1:10-11). God accepted the challenge without consulting Job.

When all our explanations for suffering are articulated, when our good reasons sound a bit too heady, and when we feel as if we have been stripped and left naked, Job's words are a good refrain: "Shall we accept good from God, and not trouble?" (2:10).

In the weaning process, God continues to bring us back to Himself alone. Job utters the cries of a man who does not understand the process he is in, but who knows he must hold on to elementary trust in God regardless of what happens.

It may seem at times that God has removed our hedge of protection and that we have been led into a stark, vacant wasteland where we appear to be easy bait, the prey of God's enemies.

J. I. Packer wrote in *Knowing God,*

> Sooner or later, the truth will be that God is now exer-
> cising His child—His consecrated child—in the ways
> of adult godliness . . . by exposing them to strong
> attacks from the world, the flesh, and the devil, so
> that their powers of resistance might grow greater,
> and their character as men of God become stronger.[9]

"Exposing" me to "strong attacks"! Whatever happened to the "still waters" He was supposed to lead me beside? Whatever happened to being carried in His bosom and the shelter of His hand? I like those peaceful, pastoral images of the Christian life. Walking through "the valley of the shadow of death" and passing "through the waters" and "through the fire" doesn't exactly sound like a stroll in the park (Psalm 23:4, Isaiah 43:2).

This is not a multiple-choice Christian life, where I get to choose the setting and images. God both purifies us and uses us to bring Him glory. Though God is our refuge, He does not shelter us from the realities of life and spiritual warfare. Though He is our shield, He does not always protect us from the piercing sting of wounds. God is not like the over-protective parent who so shelters his child that the child's growth is stunted or maladjusted. This aspect of the weaning process causes us to come to grips with the reality of faith in our Father amid the often harsh realities of life in a fallen, twisted world.

Is it possible to have a life that is too easy? Can it be that we miss something valuable if life has been too smooth?

A professor of music in Vienna said a startling thing about a pupil of his own, "She's a magnificent singer," he said, "and yet there is something lacking in her singing. Life has been too kind to her. But if one day it happened that someone broke her heart, she would be the finest singer in Europe!"[10]

In the music industry they call it "soul" or "blues." In the Christian life it is called "character."

If we don't understand that God allows us to be exercised and strengthened by exposure to greater tests, we may become alarmed when things get tough. David had the same response: "In my alarm I said, 'I am cut off from your sight!'" (Psalm 31:22). Instead of alarm, we need to remember Peter's words, "Dear friends, do not be surprised at the painful trial you are suffering, as though something strange were happening to you" (1 Peter 4:12).

Through the pain, Job knew the value of the process: "When he has tested me, I will come forth as gold" (Job 23:10). I can't think of a more heroic and challenging line than Job's cry, "Though he [God] slay me, yet will I hope in him" (13:15).

Our Signs of Confirmation
Three times God indulged Gideon's need for a sign to bolster his faith—once with the burnt offering and twice with the

fleece (Judges 6). But while en route to battle, God turned the tables. Gideon had to undergo God's weaning process as God drastically reduced his army twice. Whatever faith he had mustered prior to this campaign was quickly dissected to ensure that his heart rested in God alone, not the initial size of the army. Gideon's source of confidence had to be God, as his impressive army of thirty-two thousand was scaled down and he marched on the enemy camp with a mere three hundred.

At times, we need signs to increase our faith, and at times, we depend upon signs to confirm God's leading. Indeed, God often gives us great moments of confirmation. But there may come a season when God takes away anything that may be too much of a sign, especially when that faith is inferior and not solely anchored in Him. God may want to make sure that the object of our faith is Himself and not the sign. He wants our faith to be genuine, not magical.

Paul crossed over into Macedonia because God gave him a sign in the form of a vision (Acts 16:10). But shortly after he and Silas arrived in Macedonia, they were "severely flogged" and thrown into prison (16:23). I think if I were Silas I might have questioned Paul, "Are you sure the guy in the vision said Macedonia? Maybe you heard him wrong. After all, why would God send us here to be flogged and jailed?" Sometimes God leads us in a direction, and after we get there the signs of confirmation are gone. If we always look for signs to confirm God's leading and presence we will be unstable in our faith.

What if the missionaries mentioned earlier looked for signs of God's leading in the receptivity of people to the gospel? They would have moved on to another field too soon.

Some missionary friends of mine have a helpful line: "Don't doubt in the darkness where God has led in the light." God may call you to do something and even confirm it by a sign, but then you step out and immediately your sign of confirmation is removed or subject to second guessing. If your faith has been too dependent upon the sign, you may find yourself going through a time of weaning designed to refocus your trust.

As we will continue to explore in the next chapter, we need to learn to depend upon God alone, as Job did, trusting that He is in control of whatever happens—and that whatever happens is in His best interest for us, whether or not we see tangible evidence of this.

THIRTEEN

The Weaning Process (Part 2)

◆ ——————————————— ◆

In order to possess what you do not possess
you must go by the way of dispossession.
In order to arrive at what you are not
you must go through the way in which you are not.
T. S. Eliot
Four Quartets

◆ ——————————————— ◆

Dear friends, now we are children of God,
and what we will be has not yet been made known.
But we know that when he appears, we shall be
like him, for we shall see him as he is.
The Apostle John
1 John 3:2

◆ ——————————————— ◆

Like a weaned child is my soul within me.
King David
Psalm 131:2

◆ ——————————————— ◆

I've always liked the "Star Trek" series, both the television show and the movies. There is something heroic about going "where no man has gone before." *Star Trek II: The Wrath of Khan* opens with someone other than Captain Kirk at the helm of the starship *Enterprise*. This young replacement finds herself up against a formidable enemy who has rendered the starship virtually inoperative. As captain she is issued an ultimatum from the enemy, with death seemingly imminent. Now desperate, she is left with no way to resolve the conflict. Just at that moment the elevator doors open and in walks Captain Kirk, who signals that the exercise is over. The whole scene had been a training exercise for the cadet at the helm. The cadet, thinking she has failed, is disturbed and wants to know the solution to this exercise. But Captain Kirk explains that the exercise was not designed to "win or lose." Kirk says, "There is no resolution. It is a test of character." The cadet had passed.

Some tests are like that. They are not win-lose situations with clear-cut resolutions. They are tests of character. In our television era, half-hour situation comedies and hour-long dramas give us the impression that problems can be resolved within an hour. But in the real world, God is not in such a hurry. In fact, He takes His time. And whereas I tend to be more concerned that God somehow fix and resolve the training exercises of my life, He is much more concerned with what He can produce through testing my character.

For a long time I have felt that Paul issued a profound reminder in 1 Corinthians 13:12 when he wrote, "Now we see through a glass, darkly . . . now I know in part" (KJV); or as another version states, "Now we see but a poor reflection . . . now I know in part." We have a great wealth of revelation in Scripture for which we can be thankful. But we do not see everything clearly. We know only a part of God, and we cannot pretend to know all of His ways and reasons. This is not meant to not produce uncertainty, but trust and humility.

The weaning process reminds me that God is after something. He knows what He is after and what He is bringing about. But from the vantage point of a child, I don't always see it. That is why Scripture says, "We walk by faith, not by sight" (2 Corinthians 5:7, KJV). We must remember that God's purpose in weaning is: (1) a deeper relationship with Him, (2) a purer trust, (3) a godly contentment, and if I may add another, (4) His own glory.

We continue our discussion of the things God may wean us from.

Our Immediate Sense of God's Presence

As believers we desire a heightened sense of God's presence. We tend to misunderstand and dread the sense of His absence. A line from Thomas Merton, a Trappist monk, reminds me of Job's situation: "There are two absences of God. One is the absence that condemns us, the other an absence that sanctifies us."[1] Job was right in the middle of God's will, but it didn't appear nor feel that way from where he sat. He did not sense God's presence. "But if I go to the east, he is not there; if I go to the west, I do not find him. When he is at work in the north, I do not see him; when he turns to the south, I catch no glimpse of him" (Job 23:8-9).

Job faced the ultimate test of character. And he faced it without a great sense of God's presence. You might think that since God had ordained this predicament for Job He would go out of His way to allow Job to sense His upholding strength and cradling arms. No such warm fuzzies for Job. Nor did God send any apparent angels or special visions. Yet Job was not alone. Thomas Merton's words are poignant: "God, who is everywhere, never leaves us. Yet He seems sometimes to be present, sometimes absent. If we do not know Him well, we do not realize that He may be more present to us when He is absent than when He is present."[2]

Oswald Chambers, in commenting about Job, wrote, "A man up against things as they are feels that he has lost God, while in reality he has come face to face withHim."[3]

We all have difficulty understanding those times in life when God seems painfully absent. A man at one church told me that he didn't like the psalms because so often the writers are calling on God out of a sense of abandonment. As we talked, I realized the real reason he didn't like the psalms was that they were too close to reality. He wanted the spiritual "giants" of Scripture to attest to God always being magnificently present and profoundly inspiring. The beauty of the psalms is that they do attest to a *real* spiritual experience. That God allowed the prayers of men in desperation to be canonized shows us that even the psalms of abandonment were embraced by God as sanctified prayers of men in pursuit of Him. Christian historian Martin Marty says of the psalms, "The sense of spiritual abandonment comes with such frequency in this prayer book that all who believe in God must be ready to experience it."[4]

As evangelicals we caution each other that "feelings" should not be a gauge for the operation of theological truth in our lives. Yet as we talk about the presence of God, we betray a bit of inconsistency because we *want* a subjective presence; we *want* our hearts to be "strangely warmed." This is both good and bad. It is good to pursue God and the dynamics of His presence. However, it is foolish to panic when we don't sense the immediacy of God's presence.

We hear too much today about people wanting to "experience God." To use such language about God is to betray a basic misunderstanding of both God and Christianity that is perhaps most reflective of our times. Recent studies by sociologists have revealed that Americans today are on a relentless pursuit of self-fulfillment, individualism, and "vivid personal feeling."[5]

Christians often bring their unconscious motivations into their sincere pursuit of God. When we expect and even demand that God be a vivid personal experience we are bound to be dissatisfied. Quite simply, God is not an experience, He is a Person. God is not a feeling to be sought but a Father to be loved and obeyed. The Holy Spirit is not an experience nor an inspiring feeling. He, too, is a Person.

If we are not careful we can become "sensuous Christians." R. C. Sproul said it succinctly:

> The sensuous Christian cannot be moved to service, prayer or study unless he "feels like it." His Christian life is only as effective as the intensity of present feelings. When he experiences spiritual euphoria, he is in a whirlwind of Godly activity; when he is depressed, he is a spiritual incompetent. He constantly seeks new and fresh spiritual experiences and uses them to determine the Word of God. His "inner feelings" become the ultimate test of truth.[6]

Those times when we have the heightened sense of God's presence may not occur regularly. Oswald Chambers made some penetrating comments about how Christians view the presence of God:

> If we try to re-introduce the rare moments of inspi-
> ration, it is a sign that it is not God we want. We
> are making a fetish of the moments when God did
> come and speak, and insisting that He must do it
> again; whereas what God wants us to do is to "walk by
> faith."[7]

I have been doing some studies—including self-observa-
tion—on how we as believers experience God's strength. You
see, as a full-time pastor, I do not always sense the immediate presence of God in the form of what I would call conscious strength (I have gained confidence from the writings
of church history and some of the authors mentioned earlier
that I am not alone in this). The presence of God does not
always bring strength that is experienced as a blast of confidence, boldness, and competence. I have found that God
uses me even when I have a great sense of His absence. And
I believe that is His plan.

Paul said, "For when I am weak, then I am strong"
(2 Corinthians 12:10). We need to remember the importance
of the word *when*. Paul didn't say, "*After* I am weak, *then* I am
strong." He didn't say, "First I was weak, now I am strong."
And he didn't say, "I am weak, but God is strong." For Paul
the weakness and strength were simultaneous. He sensed
weakness in himself, but he also sensed that God was able
to show Himself strong through that weakness. It is one of
the great mysteries of the Christian life: When we are weak
in ourselves, then God can be strong in and through us. But
it still may *feel* like weakness!

On several occasions I have stepped into the pulpit with
a great sense of inadequacy and preached with a lack of
the sense of God's presence. On those days, I specifically
remember wondering how God could ever use me and the
sermon I was preaching. I would do my best, but inside I
couldn't wait until my own sermon was over and I could sit

down. Then I would sit down with a heaviness, confess my spiritual emptiness, and wonder what else I could do for a living, because I wasn't sure I could get back up there and do it again next week. And I remember getting more genuine compliments and personal interaction after those sermons than after some I preached with a great sense of God's presence. The first couple of times it happened, I remember being surprised by people's responses! God taught me some great lessons about my conscious sense of His presence and His real strength from those incidents.

Ironically, when I preached what I thought were my best sermons, I often received little response and affirmation from the congregation. God showed me the reality of "*when* I am weak, *then* I am strong." We may not sense God's presence or strength, but that does not mean it is not there.

As I've stated before, there comes a time when God weans us off our immediate sense of His presence. Perhaps it will not last long, but it will be an impressionable time as you truly learn to walk by faith, not sight. It will be a season to learn that to walk by faith at times means to walk in the absence of the sight, sound, and feeling of God. To continue Thomas Merton's thought: "In the absence that sanctifies, God empties the soul of every image that might become an idol and every concern that might stand between your face and His face."[8]

Our Preconceived Expectations of How God Will Work

Like a pinball machine flashes *tilt* when something is out of kilter, Job's friends flashed signals that he was out of whack. They had fashioned some of their own theological arithmetic, only theirs didn't add up.

Through his dialogues with people Job's test became clear: Did he still believe and trust in God even when He was not living up to Job's theological expectations of Him? There are times when we all fashion our own homespun theological terms with God that He is not ready to endorse.

The book of Job shows us that sometimes "religious

people," even good men, can unknowingly mock the purposes of God when the harsh realities of life don't fit their
nice, neat theological categories. Job's friends expounded
their spiritual-sounding explanations of the ways of God
as if their theological creeds were infallible. They show us
that well-intentioned people can operate with faulty theology when it comes to applying what they understand about
God to life situations. Sometimes armchair theologians can
make judgment calls that misrepresent God. Oswald Chambers wrote, "Most of us get touchy with God and desert Him
when He does not back up our creed."[9] If we are not careful
in our attempts to explain God we can wind up theologizing
Him right out of the picture.

One main reason why God did not give Job "answers"
was because the issue was trust. It was as if God said, "Job,
do you believe and trust in *Me* or do you merely believe
'beliefs' about Me? Can you trust Me even though your theology can not explain what is happening?" As Chambers put
it, "Though he has lost his faith in his statement of God, he
is on the way to finding God Himself."[10]

Basic, foundational theology is essential to growth. But
we must learn to recognize the preconceived expectations
we form about how God works. We must identify the ones
that are not theologically sound. To enable us to do this,
God may need to wean us so that we don't rest in "our"
theology but in Him.

When I joined the staff of one church, I had a basic job
description. I also had my expectations about what God
wanted me to do there. When things didn't work out quite
the way I had planned, it was easy, at first, to conclude that
maybe I was at the wrong church, maybe I made a mistake.
But it became clear that God had a different set of expectations for me. I was in the right place, but His purpose for
putting me there and my purpose for being there were not
in sync. I couldn't "figure God out."

This is a part of the weaning process during which we
cannot pretend to know "answers." We simply know our
Father has them, and that is enough.

These are the very times during which we may hope for a miracle, yet God in His wisdom denies us the one we hope for. And so He weans us from the spectacular and miraculous, because most of us tend to expect God to intervene in spectacular and miraculous ways. Sometimes this expectation leads to discouragement. Again, we limit our view of God by prescribing certain expectations of Him.

After Elijah's great victory over the prophets of Baal and his answered prayers for rain, he fled from evil Queen Jezebel's threat on his life. Perhaps at the heart of Elijah's discouragement was the realization that his battle was not yet over. The spectacular and the miraculous had not ensured victory. Jezebel was still on the warpath, and Elijah was discouraged.

Elijah needed to discover that God does not always deal in thunder and lightning shows. As he waited for God in the cave, God revealed that He was not in the wind that shook the mountains, nor in the earthquake, nor in the fire. This time God revealed himself to Elijah in a "still small voice," "a gentle whisper" (1 Kings 19:12, KJV, NIV).

On her way to a friend's house for pizza, a Sandi Patti tape playing in her car stereo, Bonnie Hays didn't need one more thing to go wrong on this day. Her mind was on her twenty-seven-year-old son who was dying of colon cancer. Nine years earlier her husband had died, and now it was her son—a youth pastor with a wife and child. She really believed that "God doesn't make mistakes." But she was grappling with the reality that life isn't easy for Christians. In the midst of her pain she felt alone. Who could relate to her—a mother watching her son die of cancer? Then one of her tires blew out.

"I didn't need this today," she said. She left her car and walked up to a nearby house. The people were kind enough to let her use the phone to make a call for help. There were some guests sitting at the table. In the course of the conversation, Bonnie discovered that these folks were Christians also. The mother of the house then shared, "This is a difficult time. My son is dying in the hospital."

Two strangers meeting because of a flat tire discovered that they were sisters in the Lord sharing the same pain . . . watching their sons die. Bonnie had a chance for God to use her in the midst of her own pain. She wanted these people to know that, in spite of the circumstances, God was in control.

God has a unique way of bringing divinely timed intrusions and detours into our lives. He has a creative array of methods that demonstrate why He is greater than our attempts to systematize Him, why He is unable to be contained in a box. In the weaning process, He wants us to become content to allow Him to work in any way He sees fit. Then we will become servants who can abide in trust and who can allow Him to be God.

Our Dependence upon Others' Spirituality

From what we read in the New Testament, we know that at the Corinthian church there were personality groups claiming: "I am of Paul," "I follow Apollos," "I follow Cephas." The problem continues today in Christendom. Evangelicals would never succumb to praying to a saint—even if he were Protestant. Yet the veneration and close following of some Christian celebrities bear some of the same markings of saint worship, which we frown upon.

We need to learn from and support the leaders God has placed among us. But each of us needs to develop his own personal walk with the Lord. We do not become spiritual men and women merely by reading the "right" authors or hearing the "right" preachers or attending the "right" churches. Spiritual osmosis does not happen. We cannot live out our spirituality through another's spirituality. When we grow too dependent upon the spirituality of another person, we may find that God will wean us off this dependence so that we may mature in our own spirituality.

Historically, Christian movements lose their vitality by the second and third generations of followers. The reason is that, though these followers hold to the ideas of the founders, they usually lack their spiritual fervor, piety, and burning devotion. It is a warning to us.

To read another man's devotional (especially a classic) can inspire us. But if it does not drive us to God to capture the same depth of spirituality, then we are merely enamored of another man's ideas.

Inspiration from another that does not result in personal devotion and holiness does not accomplish God's will.

Our Dependence upon the Affirmation of Others

One night not long after his conversion Paul was hiding in a basket, being lowered outside the city wall of Damascus. Perhaps this descent in the dark figuratively reminded him of his fall from the high ranks of the Jewish legal system since his conversion. He had come to town to rally the believers and instead wound up fleeing for his life. When referring to this incident in 2 Corinthians, he recalls it as a time of shame and humiliation. Paul found himself embarking on a time during which he was stripped of his group identity as a Pharisee on the one hand and held in suspicion by many in the Christian community on the other hand. Paul went through a time when his primary source of affirmation needed to come from God alone—an unusual position for anyone used to being a respected public figure.

God often needs to wean us from our need for the affirmation of our personal audience. He used this time in Paul's life to prepare him inwardly for all the conflict he would face regularly in his ministry. Paul had to come to grips early in his Christian life with the realization that his sole audience of approval was the Lord. He could not depend upon others for his strokes.

I remember the smile of an elderly woman in one church. As a young pastor scanning the congregation, I could always depend upon her encouraging smile. I knew she was pulling for me, and it gave me strength. When she died, I felt a real sense of loss. I remember several fearful walks to the pulpit in which I felt alone in those early days. God seemed to be removing a lot of props. So I began to focus on one picture in my mind. I began to imagine that a seven-foot-tall Jesus Christ was standing behind me with His hands on my shoulders as I preached. I later learned that there was a statue in Boston of Pastor Phillips Brooks with Jesus Christ standing behind him, hands on his shoulders.

Perhaps because I tend to depend upon the approval of others to give me confidence, God challenged that need early in my ministry. I remember when we stepped out to plant a church in Florida with a great sense of having nobody to lean on. We all tend to have a few people we lean on to give us a sense of not being alone. For me, it was as if God wanted me to have only Him to lean on for my affirmation and approval.

The times of weaning are occasions for growing closer and more dependent upon Christ alone and nothing else. Eugene Peterson reminds us that the process can be painful: "The transition from a sucking infant to a weaned child, from squalling baby to quiet son or daughter, is not smooth. It is stormy and noisy."[11]

We live in an age that admires and desires character but shirks the cauldron of adversity that often produces it. We want a depth of closeness to God, but we want it without the discipline of the deep inner working that precedes it. We want maturity and its benefits but without the trauma of being weaned from all our false sources of satisfaction.

Spurgeon described the necessary process toward a love for our Father that endures:

> It is not every child of God who arrives at this weanedness speedily. Some are sucklings when they ought to be fathers; others are hard to wean, and cry and fight and rage against their heavenly parent's discipline. When we think ourselves safely through the weaning, we sadly discover that the old appetites are rather wounded than slain, and we begin to cry again for the breasts which we had given up. It is easy to begin shouting before we are out of the wood, and no doubt hundreds have sung this Psalm long before

they have understood it. Blessed are those afflictions which subdue our affections, which wean us from self-sufficiency, which educate us into Christian manliness, which teach us to love God not merely when he comforts us, but even when he tries us.[12]

FOURTEEN

Full Partnership

✦

Forgive these wild and wandering cries,
confusions of a wasted youth;
Forgive them where they fail in truth,
and in thy wisdom make me wise.
Alfred Lord Tennyson
Strong Son of God, Immortal Love

✦

When I became a man,
I put childish ways behind me.
The Apostle Paul
1 Corinthians 13:11

I know the day will come for each of my children when they have to face life as adults. So I ask myself during these formative years: Am I preparing them enough for life? I believe God looks at each of us and asks the same question.

Many children grow up unprepared for adult life, the same holds true with God's children. In our case, however, it is not because God doesn't try to prepare us. More often than not the blame rests with our uncooperative spirits. Are we allowing God to prepare us for Christian maturity? Are we allowing God to prepare us for "the real world"? I'd like to share four marks of the adult Christian life by which we can determine if we are allowing our heavenly Father to develop us to spiritual maturity.

A SHIFT IN FOCUS

Children tend to be self-centered, thinking the world revolves around them. Early in the Christian's life, we are much like an infant whose focus is on "self" and what God is doing for "me." But there must come a time when the focus shifts from "what God is doing for me" to a sense of being in a joint venture with God.

Many Christians never make that shift in focus. Consequently, they are unprepared for the world in which God wants them to take their place. You can call it being a servant, or being a disciple, or maturity, or ministry-mindedness, or whatever. It doesn't matter what you call it, but it is summed up as an attitude in Philippians 2:3-4: "Do nothing out of selfish ambition or vain conceit, but in humility consider others better than yourselves. Each of you should look not only to your own interests, but also to the interests of others."

Have you noticed how some children are particularly sensitive to their parents? They seem to be much more attuned to their parents' needs and interests. My daughter is like that. Even at a young age she seemed to sense the needs and moods of my wife and me. She would say something to us at just the right time or reach out to us in her own surprising ways. In a similar way, some of God's children are more attuned to their Father. As a pastor, I have a special appreciation for those in the church who are ministry-minded. These people have learned to put others first.

I remember the Christmas morning when our children showed us that they were understanding that shift in focus. They woke Judy and me up, as they usually do, and hurried us downstairs. Spread around the Christmas tree were all their brightly colored presents waiting to be opened. Normally our children can't wait to open "their presents." But on this Christmas morning they wanted my wife and I to open the gifts they were giving to us first! They were waiting in anticipation to see our response to the gifts they bought for us. I was shocked! But that's the way we should be toward God . . . more interested in honoring Him and giving to Him than in receiving from Him.

A friend of mine who is an international coordinator of a short-term mission program told me he discovered "the two dirty words" among young Christians today. Over the years he has dealt with hundreds of people between the ages of seventeen and twenty-seven. Consistently he has found two words that make them uncomfortable: *sacrifice* and *commitment.*

The two words that capsulize a true and meaningful walk with God are the same: sacrifice and commitment. Yet even among today's Christian community these concepts have become unattractive and unappealing.

AT STAKE: THE GLORY OF GOD

There is more at stake in my walk with God than simply what I think about Him. At stake in my walk with God is the glory of God in and through my life.

What and how I think about God is important, but everything He does with me is not governed by His concern over my thoughts of Him. In other words, God's will for me is not contingent on how He in His foreknowledge knows I will respond to Him. To put it simply, as a parent there are times when I am not as concerned with what my children think of me, as I am that they obey me.

Many times in the Christian life God does not explain the details, reveal His reasoning, or show us the divine results, but His glory is at stake. The shift in focus for the believer comes when he is able to be compliant with God for a higher good: God's glory.

What do we mean by God's glory? The glory of God is not just singing at big concerts and giving people goosebumps. The glory of God is achieved when I obey Him in the quiet moments of my heart as well as when others simply take note that I am following the Lord Jesus Christ. This drama of redemption is being played out not only before men around us, but also before the heavenly host and the principalities and powers in the spiritual realm — "For our struggle is not against flesh and blood, but against the rulers, against the authorities, against the powers of this dark world and against the spiritual forces of evil in the heavenly realms" (Ephesians 6:12). We need to get into our minds that more is at stake in what is going on in and through our life than just our opinions and feelings about God.

When Job was going through his ordeal, more was at stake than simply what Job thought of God in the process. The glory of God was at stake in ways that Job did not understand until it was over (and even then he didn't understand it all). In ways that we probably don't quite grasp, at stake in our lives is the glory of God before the heavenly host and before generations of men to follow.

A WORKING RELATIONSHIP

A key aspect of maturity is developing the sense that we have a working relationship with the Father — the sense that we share a mutual task.

We are entering the family business, and God the Father is the chief owner and executive. The disciples reached this stage and Jesus said, "I no longer call you servants, because a servant does not know his master's business. Instead, I have called you friends" (John 15:15).

Working with God means that we make our lives and gifts available to His use at our own expense. The maturing believer is attuned to God's heart and God's glory.

Anna Roosevelt and her father, President Franklin Delano Roosevelt, had a special closeness. Though she had her own life and her own profession, her sensitivity to him led her to resign her own job and move into the White House to help him during the last sixteen months leading up to his death in April 1945. With her father confined to a wheelchair, Anna became increasingly involved in the workings of his inner circle. She had an effect on her father and the mood of the White House that her mother, Eleanor (who was rather humorless and weighed down with responsibility), never did.

Anna did it by serving. Eleanor wrote, "Anna's presence was the greatest possible help to my husband. . . . She saw and talked to people whom Franklin was too busy to see. . . . She also took over the supervision of his food. . . . She brought to all her contacts a gaiety and buoyancy that made everybody feel just a little happier because she was around."[1]

Anna's loving relationship with her father extended into a joyful working relationship. She shows us her attitude in these words:

> In my work for him I never had an official job or title or salary. . . . I was there all the time and it was easy for Father to tell someone to "ask Anna to do that. . . ."
>
> It was immaterial to me whether my job was helping plan the 1944 campaign, pouring tea for General de Gaulle or filling Father's empty cigarette case. All that mattered was relieving a greatly overburdened man of a few details of work and trying to make his life as pleasant as possible when a few moments opened up for relaxation.[2]

Anna loved her father, and out of that love, she served him and sacrificed for him.

It seems that due to current excesses we have created the mistaken notion of the "privileged servant of God"—one who because of his deeper commitment and service reaps more material benefits and is privileged to special treatment by God and man. Christian history, missions, and Scripture give quite a different picture. Those who were more committed to serving God were more likely to be those whom God called upon to make the biggest sacrifices in material benefits, external comforts, and earthly security. They were privileged, but in a much more internal and eternal way.

Paul's service for Christ meant that he would be "underprivileged" so that others could be blessed:

We always carry around in our body the death of Jesus, so that the life of Jesus may also be revealed in our body. For we who are alive are always being given over to death for Jesus' sake, so that his life may be revealed in our mortal body. So then, death is at work in us, but life is at work in you. (2 Corinthians 4:10-12)

So I will very gladly spend for you everything I have and expend myself as well. If I love you more, will you love me less? (2 Corinthians 12:15)

GOD TAKES LIBERTIES WITH OUR LIVES

As my children grow older I expect more of them. I expect them to be more responsible, more giving, more sensitive to the needs and feelings of others. If I did not expect those things they would not grow into healthy adults. I also realize that as a parent, I ask my children to do things that I wouldn't ask other children to do, simply because they are *my* children. I have a certain liberty with my children that I don't have with others.

Another key step of maturity is our willingness to allow God to take liberties with our life. Being committed to God and the Great Commission means that God may take liberties with our life that He might not take with the less committed and the less mature. As our level of trust in God's goodness and wisdom grows, God knows He can use us with more freedom. What a great privilege!

Once again, Job is instructive. His outstanding character didn't mean he had a sign that read: *Hands off. Privileged Servant of God.* On the contrary, it gave God the liberty to allow his life to be tested for the glory of God. Job's testing was spiritual warfare. At stake was the glory of God.

Sometimes God wants to use certain lives for specific purposes. In particular, He used the lives of His prophets as object lessons. God asked Jeremiah not to marry (Jeremiah 16:1-2). Ezekiel married, but the Lord took his wife and told him that he would "be a sign" (Ezekiel 24:15-27). God asked Hosea to marry an adulterous woman (Hosea 1). These servants' whole lives became object lessons, signs pointing to God. The list could go on and on of people who gave God the liberty to use their lives as He desired.

- ◆ Have you ever thought that what God is doing in your life at certain times is more for others than for you? Have you considered that God may want to use your life as a flesh-and-blood object lesson for others? Many times as I have watched what God was doing in another person's life, their testimony has ministered to me.
- ◆ Have you made the crucial shift in focus that will enable God to use you as a servant?
- ◆ Do you realize that more is at stake in your walk with God than your own thought life?
- ◆ Do you have a working relationship with God in which you sense you share a mutual task with God?
- ◆ Are you prepared to grant God the liberty to use your life as He chooses to bring Himself glory and to advance the Kingdom?

Scripture calls us to a deep level of maturity. Paul talks about growing up by putting away childish things (1 Corinthians 13:11). He challenges people to think as adults (1 Corinthians 14:20). Hebrews exhorts us to "leave the elementary teachings . . . and go on to maturity" (6:1).

It is on the road to maturity that we realize the benefits of full partnership with the Father. To have the sense of co-laboring with God and being a part of what He is doing is its own reward. There is a joy in sacrifice because in the process God the Father reveals Himself to the heart of His child.

In My Father's Footsteps

*I rejoice in your success, father—nothing is more
precious to me in the world. What medal of honor
brighter to his children than a father's growing glory?
Or a child's to his proud father?*
Sophocles
"Antigone"

*As for me, I will behold thy face in righteousness:
I shall be satisfied, when I awake, with thy likeness.*
King David
Psalm 17:15, KJV

Over the years people have told me how much I look like my father. My three brothers and I have taken turns resembling him at different stages. As I thumb through old pictures of my dad I'm amazed how much I resemble him now.

But it's not only how much we look alike. When I was a kid, I remember looking through my father's old scrapbook of drawings he'd made when he was a youth. He had kept it for years, though it has since been lost. From him I inherited artistic ability, and today, my children look through *my* old scrapbook of drawings I made over twenty-five years ago!

When people used to ask me where I learned carpentry and woodworking, I didn't have a good answer. I wasn't trained in it, nor did I do much study in those areas. I've since realized that I learned it from the years of being around my father. I guess I caught more than he actually taught me. The same is true for my knowledge of photography and handy skills in wiring and electricity, wallpapering, and other areas.

I remember picking up a piece of scrap paper on my workbench and finding some measurements scrawled on it. I was immediately reminded of my dad. *That's Dad's hand-writing!* I thought. Of course I knew it wasn't; it was mine. But now even my handwriting resembles his.

Sometimes when I hear myself laughing, I am reminded of my father's laugh. I know that I sound like him.

Fathers (and mothers) pass on many things to their children. God has designed our genes that way. Just as we resemble our earthly fathers, God intends us to resemble Him more and more. Our spiritual inheritance is not only a heavenly home, it is God passing on to us His nature and character here and now. We have spiritual as well as physical genes.

I remember a Barbara Walters special in which she interviewed leading Hollywood stars. Each of them seemed to become more real and let the walls down when they talked about their fathers. I remember one star in particular. At the time he was one of the hot, new, macho-man types. As he talked about his father, his eyes teared and his voice quivered as he said affectionately, "I was going to make that man proud of me." I was moved because I realized many of us feel that same way. I also realized that I have that same motivation toward my heavenly Father.

"I want to make God proud of me." There is a righteous and noble way to say those words as a child of God. They are words in keeping with the call in Scripture to walk worthy of your calling, to press on toward the high calling of God, to let men see your progress, to fight the good fight of faith. They are the words that will result in our Father embracing us and saying, "Well done, good and faithful servant" (Matthew 25:21).

I remember a scene in a television commercial some

time back. I don't remember what it was for, but it moved me. A young man was receiving some recognition for his recent achievement. Later, at an informal gathering, an older, distinguished man said to him, "I'm proud of you, son." Then they embraced.

Some fathers would never think to say those words to their children. Some children never hear those words from a parent. But they yearn to. I was moved because I believe God says that to you and me. Jesus' prayer in John 17 tells us that He is proud of His disciples. There is a righteous and noble sense to realizing that God at times says to you and me, "I am proud of you, son," or "I am proud of you, daughter."

The parent-child bond is powerful. How much more powerful it is between God and His children! We need to tap into the deep roots of our parental bond with God. We need to draw out all the emotional richness that gives vitality and passion to our relationship with this utterly holy yet remarkably down-to-earth Father. Our Emmanuel, "God with us," dwells with us in ways that are beyond our comprehension. We need to be motivated in a righteous and wholesome sense by the words, "I want to make God my Father proud of me." And we need to be motivated by the knowledge that God is a Father who will embrace us with the words, "I'm proud of you, son." That's what the bond of father and child is all about.

In one of the 1988 NCAA college basketball Final Four playoff games there were two notable fathers watching their sons follow in their footsteps. The Kansas University Jayhawks were playing the Oklahoma Sooners. On the court were Danny Manning, college "player of the year," and Scooter Barry. On the sidelines was Danny's dad, one of the Kansas coaches. In the stands was Scooter's dad, Rick Barry, a former NBA star. As the camera focused on these dads at various times in the game you could see they were living those moments with their sons. These proud fathers appeared pleased that it was their sons' turn to face the big-game pressure and shine.

Championship games often come down to making free throws in the last moments of the game. This game was no exception. During the final two minutes with the game on the line, both sons had to shoot free throws. In both instances, the dad watching appeared more nervous than the son who stood at the foul line. Because both of these fathers had played basketball, they had been there before, and they knew the pressure their sons faced. They were reliving it through their sons' experience. And when the free throws went through the hoop, no one was more excited than those two fathers.

I couldn't help seeing a picture of God the Father in those two dads. Sometimes God must be on the edge of His seat in anticipation with me in my moments of pressure. God the supportive Father cheering me on, agonizing with me, and sharing in my triumphs and joys.

Jesus used the parables of the lost sheep, the lost coin, and the prodigal son to emphasize the joyous celebration of God and the angels over lost sinners who are found. When we go to be with the Lord, we will celebrate the joyous reunion at "the wedding supper of the Lamb" (Revelation 19:9). When He finds us He rejoices, and when He brings us into eternity He rejoices. Like two bookends, our lives are framed by the joyous celebration of God. In between, it is our turn to walk in Jesus' footsteps.

I was reminded of my bond with God my Father once again quite unexpectedly while watching "live" one of those rare moments in televised sports. It was the 1987 Wimbledon men's championship finals. Twenty-two-year-old Australian Pat Cash had just won in straight sets over Ivan Lendel. Cash, a long-shot winner seeded eleventh, had beaten the number one player in the world. Half way up in the stands Pat's father, a former football player—a large, exuberant man—was cheering with his arms in the air as his son walked off the court. British protocol at Wimbledon dictates that the winner first is congratulated by royalty right there at the side of the court. It is usually a five-to-ten-minute wait before the winner can greet his family and coaches. But Pat Cash had other plans. As he left the court, he went straight for his dad.

The camera followed him as he climbed the stands over seats and barriers to the tenth row where his dad stood waiting. The two embraced, the big, burly father and his slender, young son. No one thought it disrespectful. On the contrary, it was refreshingly spontaneous. In that moment, everyone in the stadium and everyone watching on television could relate . . . those who had good fathers, those who had poor fathers, and those who had no fathers. In that moment, we were all reminded of how it can be. A father and his child can share a powerful, emotional bond.

As I watched it I saw more than a tennis player and his father. The truth is, it can be that way between us and God our Father. The scene became a window into the spiritual dynamics of God and His children. I pictured our exuberant heavenly Father cheering us on, His arms thrust in the air in victory. I saw you and me with one thing on our minds: making a beeline straight to our Father over stairs and barriers, forgoing all the congratulations of men. I imagined the bear-hug embrace of our expectant Father to whom we owe everything. And I heard our proud Father whispering in our ears the words we've longed to hear but by this time probably don't even need to be said, "Well done . . . My child."

Endnotes

CHAPTER ONE – A SECRET YEARNING

1. Elyce Wakerman, *Father Loss* (Garden City, NY: Doubleday, 1984), pages 138-139.
2. Dr. Ken Druck with James C. Simmons, *The Secrets Men Keep* (New York: Ballantine Books, 1987), page 5.
3. Druck, pages 38-39.
4. Louie Anderson, *Dear Dad* (New York: Viking, 1989), page 21.
5. Judith Arcana, *Every Mother's Son* (Garden City, NY: Anchor Press, 1983), page 142.
6. Suzanne Fields, *Like Father, Like Daughter* (Boston, MA: Little, Brown & Co., 1983), page 9 (emphasis added).

7. Fields, page 9.
8. Fields, page 9.
9. Fields, page 10.
10. Fields, page 11.
11. Fields, pages 8-9.
12. Wakerman, page 13 (emphasis added).
13. Wakerman, page 264.
14. Wakerman, page 271.
15. Wakerman, page 270.
16. Charles Dickens, *Dombey and Son* (New York: Simon & Schuster, 1968), quoted in Fields, page 63.
17. Alexander Towle, ed., *Fathers* (New York: Simon & Schuster, 1986), page 222.

CHAPTER TWO — GOD IS A DAD, TOO!

1. Alexandra Towle, ed., *Fathers* (New York: Simon & Schuster, 1986), pages 205-206.
2. Elyce Wakerman, *Father Loss* (Garden City, NY: Doubleday, 1984), page 250.
3. Wakerman, page 251.
4. Wakerman, page 251.
5. Wakerman, page 252.
6. *Orlando Sentinel*, 6 September 1989, sec. B, page 6.
7. *Orlando Sentinel*, 2 July 1989, sec. C, page 1.
8. Towle, page 251.

CHAPTER THREE — ABBA, FATHER

1. Quoted in *Creative Suffering*, Paul Tournier (San Francisco, CA: Harper & Row, 1983), page 31.
2. Quoted in *Orphans: Real and Imaginary*, Eileen Simpson (New York: Weidenfeld and Nicolson, 1987), page 19.
3. Simpson, page 172.
4. Tournier, page 10.
5. J. I. Packer, *Knowing God* (Downers Grove, IL: InterVarsity, 1973), pages 187-188.

6. The references are: adoption, Romans 8:15,23; Galatians 4:5; Ephesians 1:5—inheritance, Ephesians 1:14, 5:5; Colossians 1:12, 3:24; Hebrews 9:15; 1 Peter 1:4—heirs, Romans 8:17; Galatians 3:29, 4:7; Ephesians 3:6; 1 Peter 3:7.
7. Francis Lyall, *Slaves, Citizens, Sons* (Grand Rapids MI: Zondervan, 1984), page 120.
8. Lyall, page 121.
9. Lyall, page 86.
10. Lyall, page 83.
11. Lyall, page 104.
12. Lyall, page 111.
13. Lyall, page 109.
14. *Institutes 2.157.*
15. Packer, page 204.
16. D. A. Carson, *Matthew*, vol. 8, *The Expositors' Bible Commentary*, Frank Gaebelein, gen. ed. (Grand Rapids, MI: Zondervan, 1984), page 161.
17. The references are: Romans 1:7; 1 Corinthians 1:3; 2 Corinthians 1:2; Galatians 1:1,3-4; Ephesians 1:2-3; Philippians 1:2; Colossians 1:2; 1 Thessalonians 1:1,3; 2 Thessalonians 1:1-2; 1 Timothy 1:2; 2 Timothy 1:2; Titus 1:4; Philemon 3; 1 Peter 1:2; 1 John 1:2-3; 2 John 3; Jude 1.
18. Herman Bavinck, *The Doctrine of God* (Grand Rapids, MI: Baker Book House, 1977), pages 109-110.
19. Packer, page 182.
20. Packer, page 182.

CHAPTER FOUR—PARENTAL HANGOVER

1. J. B. Phillips, *Your God Is Too Small* (New York: Macmillan, 1972), page 19.
2. Paul D. Meier, *Christian Child-Rearing and Personality Development* (Grand Rapids, MI: Baker Book House, 1981), page 30.
3. Meier, page 30.
4. Meier, page 31.

5. C. S. Lewis, *The Joyful Christian* (New York: Macmillan, 1984), page 38.
6. Phillips, page 20.
7. Floyd McClung, Jr., *The Father Heart of God* (Eugene, OR: Harvest House, 1985), page 14.
8. Oswald Chambers, *The Place of Help* (Fort Washington, PA: Christian Literature Crusade, 1975), page 227.
9. Phillips, page 22.

CHAPTER FIVE — A FATHER WITH HIS HEART ON HIS SLEEVE

1. Colin Brown, ed., *New International Dictionary of New Testament Theology*, vol. 1 (Grand Rapids, MI: Zondervan, 1979), page 614.
2. J. I. Packer, *Knowing God* (Downers Grove, IL: Inter-Varsity, 1973), page 204.
3. *Orlando Sentinel*, 18 June 1989, sec. A, page 3 (emphasis added).
4. Lorraine Hansberry, *A Raisin in the Sun* (New York: Signet, 1988), page 145.

CHAPTER SIX — FATHER KNOWS BEST

1. Russell Baker, *Growing Up* (New York: Congdon & Weed, 1982), page 61.
2. Bruce Narramore, *Parenting with Love and Limits* (Grand Rapids, MI: Zondervan, 1979).
3. Quoted in *Papa, My Father*, Leo Buscaglia (New York: William Morrow, 1989), page 41.
4. Quoted in *Classic Sermons on Suffering*, ed. Warren Wiersbe (Grand Rapids, MI: Kregel, 1984), page 87.
5. *Trinity's Wellspring* (Deerfield, IL: Trinity Evangelical Divinity School, Summer 1989), page 6.
6. *Trinity's Wellspring*, page 14.
7. Michael Quoist, *The Prayers of Life* (New York: Gill and Macmillan, 1963), quoted in *Fear No Evil*, David Watson (Wheaton, IL: Harold Shaw, 1984), page 132.

CHAPTER SEVEN—THIS IS GOING TO HURT ME
MORE THAN IT HURTS YOU

1. There is a helpful discussion of this in *Freedom from Guilt*, Bruce Narramore and Bill Counts (Irvine, CA: Harvest House, 1974), pages 22-26.
2. Narramore, page 21.
3. Signe Hammer, *Passionate Attachments* (New York: Rawson & Associates, 1982), page 22.
4. Gleason Archer, *Theological Wordbook of the Old Testament*, vol. 1 (Chicago, IL: Moody Press, 1980), page 386.
5. Alexander MacLaren, *Expositions of Holy Scripture*, vol. 16 (Grand Rapids, MI: Baker Book House, 1984), pages 218-219.
6. *Orlando Sentinel*, 18 December 1989, sec. A, page 9.
7. Malcolm Muggeridge, *A Twentieth Century Testimony* (Nashville, TN: Thomas Nelson, 1978), page 35.

CHAPTER EIGHT—MY DAD'S BIGGER
THAN YOUR DAD

1. Suzanne Fields, *Like Father, Like Daughter* (Boston, MA: Little, Brown & Co., 1983), page 3.
2. Elisabeth Elliot, *The Savage My Kinsman* (Ann Arbor, MI: Servant Books, 1981), page 9.
3. Quoted in *Fear No Evil*, David Watson (Wheaton, IL: Harold Shaw, 1985), pages 135-136.
4. Lina Sandel, "Day by Day," in *Hymns for the Family of God*, ed. Fred Brock (Nashville, TN: Paragon Associates, 1976), #102.

CHAPTER NINE—THE BREADWINNER
AND THE BREAD OF LIFE

1. *U.S. News & World Report*, 7 August 1989, page 49.
2. *U.S. News*, page 49.
3. *U.S. News*, page 49.

CHAPTER TEN—A FATHER WHO NEVER LETS GO

1. John R. W. Stott, *The Epistles of John* (Grand Rapids, MI: Eerdmans, 1979), page 96.

CHAPTER ELEVEN—GROWING PAINS

1. Dr. Dan Kiley, *The Peter Pan Syndrome* (New York: Hearst Corporation/Avon Books, 1988).
2. Oswald Chambers, *The Place of Help* (Fort Washington, PA: Christian Literature Crusade, 1975), page 100.

CHAPTER TWELVE—THE WEANING PROCESS (PART 1)

1. Artur Weiser, *The Psalms* (Philadelphia, PA: Westminster Press, 1962), page 777.
2. Eugene Peterson, *A Long Obedience in the Same Direction* (Downers Grove, IL: InterVarsity, 1980), page 150.
3. Charles H. Spurgeon, *The Treasury of David*, vol. VI (Grand Rapids, MI: Zondervan, 1950), page 137.
4. Peterson, page 152.
5. Oswald Chambers, *Christian Discipline*, vol. III (London: Marshall, Morgan, and Scott, 1978), page 93.
6. A. W. Tozer, *The Best of A. W. Tozer* (Grand Rapids, MI: Baker Book House, 1986), page 48.
7. J. B. Phillips, *The Price of Success* (Wheaton, IL: Harold Shaw, 1984), page 9.
8. Larry Crabb, *Inside Out* (Colorado Springs, CO: NavPress, 1988), page 84.
9. J. I. Packer, *Knowing God* (Downers Grove, IL: InterVarsity, 1973), page 225.
10. James S. Stewart, "Wearing the Thorns as a Crown," in *Classic Sermons on Suffering*, ed. Warren Wiersbe (Grand Rapids, MI: Kregel, 1984), page 92.

CHAPTER THIRTEEN—THE WEANING PROCESS (PART 2)

1. Thomas Merton, *No Man Is an Island* (New York: Harcourt, Brace, Jovanovich, 1978), page 237.

2. Merton, page 237.
3. Oswald Chambers, *Baffled to Fight Better* (London: Marshall, Morgan, and Scott, 1977), page 18.
4. Martin Marty, *A Cry of Absence* (San Francisco, CA: Harper & Row, 1983), page 126.
5. Refer to *Habits of the Heart*, Robert Bellah, R. Madsen, et al. (New York: Harper & Row, 1985).
6. R. C. Sproul, *Knowing Scripture* (Downers Grove, IL: InterVarsity, 1977), page 27.
7. Oswald Chambers, *My Utmost for His Highest* (New York: Dodd, Mead, & Co., 1963), page 122.
8. Merton, page 237.
9. Chambers, *Baffled to Fight Better*, page 9.
10. Chambers, *Baffled to Fight Better*, page 54.
11. Eugene Peterson, *A Long Obedience in the Same Direction* (Downers Grove, IL: InterVarsity, 1980), page 151.
12. Charles H. Spurgeon, *The Treasury of David*, vol. VI (Grand Rapids, MI: Zondervan, 1950), page 138.

CHAPTER FOURTEEN — FULL PARTNERSHIP

1. Bernard Asbell, ed., *Mother and Daughter: The Letters of Eleanor and Anna Roosevelt* (New York: Coward, McCann, & Geoghegan, 1982), page 176.
2. Asbell, pages 175-176.